BRETT FAVRE

A Packer Fan's Tribute

Revised and Expanded Edition with Fan Tributes

BRETT FAVRE

A Packer Fan's Tribute
Revised and Expanded Edition with Fan Tributes

Tom Kertscher

CUMBERLAND HOUSE
PUBLISHING INC.

BRETT FAVRE: A PACKER FAN'S TRIBUTE
PUBLISHED BY CUMBERLAND HOUSE PUBLISHING
431 Harding Industrial Drive
Nashville, TN 37211

Cover design: Gore Studio, Inc.
Photos: Jim Biever
Book design: Stacie Bauerle

Library of Congress Cataloging-in-Publication Data

Kertscher, Tom, 1961-
  Brett Favre : a Packer fan's tribute / Tom Kertscher. — 2nd ed.
    p. cm.
  ISBN-13: 978-1-58182-608-1 (hardcover : alk. paper)
  ISBN-10: 1-58182-608-7 (hardcover : alk. paper)
 1. Favre, Brett. 2. Football players—United States—Biography. 3. Football players—United States—Pictorial works. 4. Green Bay Packers (Football team) I. Title.
  GV939.F29K47 2007
  796.33092--dc22
  [B]
                                                                    2007009666

Printed in China
1 2 3 4 5 6 7—12 11 10 09 08 07 06

For my parents, Jim and Barbara Kertscher

*Who made sports a part of my life and
taught me to look for the good in people.*

CONTENTS

★★★★★★★★★★★

ACKNOWLEDGEMENTS

Many authors say a book would not be possible were it not for so-and-so. In the case of *Brett Favre: A Packer Fan's Tribute* it is an absolute truth.

On my day job, I'm a reporter for the *Milwaukee Journal Sentinel*. But I cover news, so as far as sports goes, I'm just a fan. That means that without the work of many sports reporters—for the game accounts, quotations, statistics, etc.—there would be no book.

I want to give special recognition to the reporters whose stories I relied on most: Bob McGinn and Tom Silverstein of the *Milwaukee Journal Sentinel*, and Tom Oates, Jason Wilde, and Kent Youngblood of the *Wisconsin State Journal* in Madison. Although fewer in number, articles by Peter King of *Sports Illustrated* and Don Pierson of the *Chicago Tribune* also were invaluable.

I used information from articles by many other reporters, as well, and want to name some of them here: Cliff Christl, Gary D'Amato, Dale Hofmann, Lori Nickel, and Bob Wolfley of the *Journal Sentinel*; Brad Zimanek of the *Journal Sentinel's* sister publication, *Packer Plus*; Vic Feuerherd and Rob Hernandez of the *State Journal*; Arnie Stapleton of The Associated Press; Chris Havel of the *Green Bay Press-Gazette*; and Todd Finkelmeyer and Rob Schultz of *The* (Madison) *Capital Times*.

Much gratitude goes to Packers team photographer Jim Biever, who provided the photographs for this book. It was a privilege and a joy to work with such an accommodating and humble man.

Special thanks go to Greg J. Borowski, my *Journal Sentinel* colleague, fellow author, and valued friend, for his advice, assistance, and encouragement.

THE BEST

★★★★★★★★★★

I go through life saying,
"What can I do on the football field
to make people say,
'Now, that guy's good.
Not just because he can throw touchdown passes
but because he's a great leader,
he busted his ass,
he was always there,
you could always depend on him,
he was tough.'"

—Brett Favre

I **admire** Brett Favre for all those reasons: outstanding player, true leader, gave his all, dependable, tough. But even with all of Favre's greatness—and I am speaking as a lifelong Green Bay Packers fan here—I don't use the word admire lightly.

For those of us born too late for the Vince Lombardi days, it hasn't been easy being a fan of pro sports. Many of the best players are selfish and short-sighted. Year after year, they jump from team to team, concerned more about money than winning, seeming to care not at all about the fans. And yet, even those who make millions can't do something as simple as hustle on every play, or play when hurt. If that type of player didn't disgust you so much, you'd feel sorry for him. He's blessed with a great career and a personal fortune—but because he chased after the money so much, after he retires, you can't even identify him with a single team.

You wonder if today's players ever look ahead: When they get old, will it be the millions or the memories that will make them happy?

Favre has his money, but he knows that the memories will be his true treasure—just as they are for his fans.

It's true, I suppose, that Brett Favre would not have forged the relationship he did with his fans if he hadn't returned the Packers to Super Bowl glory. Winning may not be everything, but it's an awful big thing.

At the same time, I know that Favre wouldn't have meant as much to me if it weren't for his many other qualities. And I believe many Packer fans feel the same way.

The victory in Super Bowl XXXI and Favre's three consecutive Most Valuable Player awards were special not merely because he achieved them, but because of the way he did it. No quarterback ever put his body on the line more for his team—for his fans—than Favre did. He was without peer when it came to playing all-out on every play, never giving up in a game. And through all the years, he had as much fun on the football field as any kid could.

He also stayed simple and humble—a T-shirt and flip-flops, not a tailored suit and sunglasses.

He was a superstar you truly could imagine having a beer with.

Most importantly, Favre did all those things as a Packer (after, thank God, he bombed out in his rookie season in Atlanta). He could have left Green Bay any number of times. Or he could have stayed but demanded so much money that he would have crippled the Packers. Favre certainly tested the patience of his fans after the 2005 season, when he continued to delay a decision on whether he would retire. But in the end, he stayed a Packer. Favre realized that you only get one shot at a career in the NFL, and that there is no sports franchise more special than the Green Bay Packers. He played in one place and became the most beloved Packer of all time.

In short: Favre did it the way we Packer fans would have done it, if we had ever had the chance.

In this day and age, that's truly something to admire.

—Tom Kertscher

CHAPTER 1
INSTANT STAR

✭✭✭✭✭✭✭✭✭✭

*I think it was the beginning
of something great in Green Bay.*

—Brett Favre
on his first
game-winning
touchdown pass

Brett Favre came to the Green Bay Packers without fanfare—but not without a reputation.

His rookie season in Atlanta had been a washout.

"All he did was drink beer and eat chicken wings for a year," said Falcons Head Coach Jerry Glanville. "He looked like the Pillsbury Doughboy."

Not that many fans probably noticed. As the third-string quarterback, Favre threw exactly four passes during the 1991 season. He completed none, and two were intercepted.

Even worse, according to Glanville, Favre was uncoachable. Among other things, he failed to show up for the team photo.

"I got trapped behind a car wreck," Favre claimed.

"You are a car wreck," Glanville snapped.

And yet, in the eyes of Ron Wolf, Brett Favre was the man to return the Packers to glory.

At Southern Mississippi University, Favre had attracted attention, and even pie-in-the-sky Heisman Trophy talk, with his gutsy play and upset victories. After his senior season failed to meet expectations, Favre dropped a few notches with some NFL scouts—but not with Wolf, who was director of player personnel for the New York Jets. A key reason was a man named Famous Coleman, an assistant coach at Southern Mississippi, who made it a point to show Wolf tapes of Favre's more impressive junior season. Wolf was convinced—he had to get Favre.

Famous Coleman. He deserves a place in the Packers Hall of Fame.

Whatever was on that tape, it convinced Wolf that he had found a player who could transform the proud, but lately pitiful, Green Bay Packers. Wolf had come to Green Bay after Favre's rookie season in the NFL.

"All I could think of is that, about once a generation, a quarterback comes along who has this particular quality, and that's the ability to make it seem as though the whole field is tilting one way whenever he's out there," Wolf said.

That epiphany, next to the hiring of Vince Lombardi, would become the most important inspiration in the history of the franchise.

On February 10, 1992, less than three months into his new job as the Packers general manager, Wolf seized his opportunity.

He traded a coveted first-round draft choice for the NFL version of the Pillsbury Doughboy.

No one was impressed.

"I said, 'OK. Whatever,'" Favre recalled of being informed of the trade. "And I finished my crawfish and my beer."

No champagne glasses were raised in Packerland, either. Fans wondered whether the Packers had blown another chance to rebuild the team, giving up a top draft pick for a no-name. Even team President Bob Harlan couldn't get excited—he hadn't heard of Favre until Wolf told him he was about to make the trade.

Talk about a lone Wolf.

"'Have you lost your mind?' was what most people said," he recalled.

Favre turned the trade into one of the greatest in the history of sports. But even he didn't blame the early doubters.

"It looked like a good deal for Atlanta," he said. Who would have known it would work out the way it did?

✶✶✶✶✶✶✶✶✶✶

Favre taking a snap during a practice in August 1992, prior to his first season with the Packers.

Like Favre, the Packers had performed miserably in 1991. They finished 4–12, failing to make the playoffs for the eighth straight year.

For Packer fans, nothing would ever erase the memories of the team's three consecutive world championships. But those memories—now a generation old—were starting to fade.

Hope surged during the off season when, a month before acquiring Favre, Wolf hired Mike Holmgren as head coach. As an assistant in San Francisco, Holmgren had helped the 49ers win back-to-back Super Bowls.

Beginning their Packer careers together, Wolf, Holmgren, and Favre would make new championship memories.

Initially, Holmgren kept Don "Majik" Majkowski, the blonde-locked, silver-Mercedes-driving quarterback, as his starter. But he installed Favre as second string and believed he would get a chance to show his stuff at some point during the '92 season.

The wait was short. In game three against the Cincinnati Bengals, Favre and an even less-heralded player—wide receiver Kitrick Taylor—hooked up to create one of the greatest moments in Lambeau Field history.

Quarterback Don Majkowski being carried off the field after Cincinnati Bengals lineman Tim Krumrie sacked him on September 19, 1992. The injury to Majkowski's ankle gave Favre his first chance to become the Packers' starting quarterback.

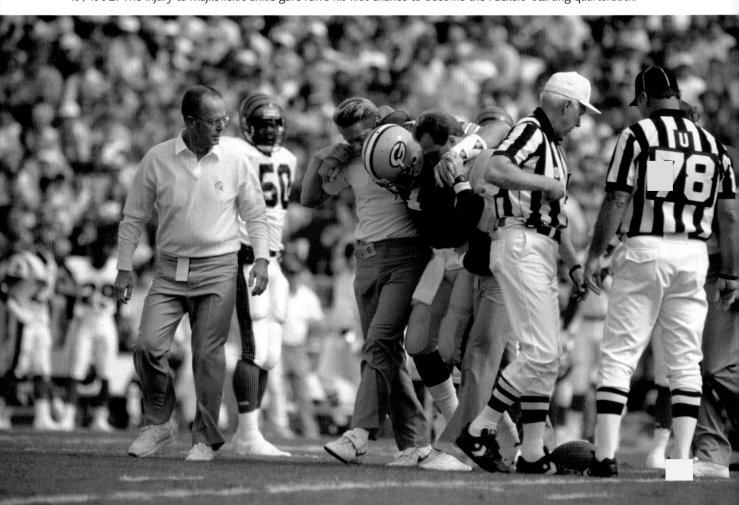

"Everyone, from that point on, felt like I could play," Favre said.

Early in the game, 275-pound defensive tackle Tim Krumrie, a former Wisconsin Badger, sacked Majkowski and landed on his left ankle, straining the ligaments. An overheated Favre went in.

"I felt like I had just taken a laxative. I was shaking all over," Favre recalled. "Thank goodness I managed to hold it in until the whole thing was over with."

The hyper-intensity showed. Favre tripped over his teammates, tried to call a timeout when he couldn't, called the wrong formations and threw to the wrong receivers. In the first three quarters, he fumbled four times and was sacked five times.

Favre looked like he had spent the last season gulping beer and chomping down chicken wings.

He also took some hard hits—which apparently helped.

"The more I got hit, the easier things got," he said. "They knock all of the stupidity out of you."

Despite Favre's near-meltdown, the Packers kept the game close. Rookie running back Edgar Bennett began to sense something special was happening.

Favre scanning the field after taking over for Majkowski in the Bengals game.

"When the Majik Man went down, everyone was like, 'What are we going to do now?'" Bennett recalled. "But as soon as Brett took the field, the confidence was there. I don't think a player in that huddle doubted him."

Favre eventually settled down. And in the fourth quarter, as he would do so many times in his career, he took control.

With less than nine minutes left and the Bengals leading 20–10, Favre drove the team 88 yards in eight plays. He completed 5-of-6 passes, including a 5-yard touchdown to star receiver Sterling Sharpe, making the score 20–17.

Green Bay stopped the Bengals on their next possession. But hopes dimmed after Terrell Buckley—who earlier had scored on a 58-yard punt return in what was his first NFL game—fumbled the punt. The Bengals recovered and went on to kick a field goal, extending their lead to 23–17.

The Packers had one final chance—but hurt themselves again.

On the ensuing kickoff, rookie receiver Robert Brooks caught the ball and clumsily stepped out of bounds at the 8-yard line—forcing the Packers to go 92 yards in 67 seconds, without any timeouts.

Favre didn't blink. He completed a short pass, then drove the Packers across midfield by hitting Sharpe for 42 yards. Sharpe re-injured his bruised ribs on the play, however, and had to be replaced by Taylor, a newly signed free agent. Taylor would later recall what Favre had said in the huddle: "We're going to score. We're going to get in the end zone."

From the Bengals' 35-yard line, Taylor ran the same "go" route that Sharpe had just run. This time, Favre pump-faked before firing a laser down the right sideline that didn't rise more than 12 feet off the ground. Taylor snatched it and dashed into the north end zone, tying the game at 23 with 13 seconds left.

With Favre holding for the first time, Chris Jacke added the extra point, and the euphoric Packers claimed a 24–23 win.

This is what Packer fans had been yearning for: a fearless, blue-collar quarterback with a big heart who could win respect, and games, by going all out on every play.

After the win, Favre ran around the field looking for someone to hug. He ended up head-butting guard Ron Hallstrom with his helmet and split open his forehead. "I had blood running down my face but I didn't feel it," Favre said.

Favre admitted later he had been so pumped during the final series that he thought his winning TD pass might have gone into the seats. "When I threw it, I closed my eyes. I was just waiting for a cheer," he said.

Taylor felt the magic in what would be his only NFL touchdown reception.

"After I caught it, I didn't hear anything. I was on a natural high," he said.

The legend had begun.

Favre getting congratulations on his last-second game-winning touchdown pass to Kitrick Taylor, shown in the background, which gave the Packers a 24–23 come-from-behind victory over the Bengals. He suffered the small cut between his eyes moments earlier when he head-butted offensive lineman Ron Hallstrom while celebrating the TD.

With Majkowski still ailing, Favre made his first start the next week, in a 17–3 win over the undefeated Pittsburgh Steelers. Majkowski never started another game for the Packers.

Behind Favre, the Packers finished '92 at 9–7—their second-best record in 20 years and good for second place in the NFC Central. They won five straight games for the first time since 1966, during Lombardi's reign as coach.

Favre set a team record by completing 64.1 percent of his passes and, at twenty-three, became the youngest player ever to play in the Pro Bowl.

A march toward the Hall of Fame had started with a touchdown pass to a receiver named Kitrick Taylor.

"As I was walking off the field," Favre said of the Bengals game, "I knew I'd have to be dead before I'd ever come out of the lineup again."

★★★★★★★★★★

*When all those around you have doubt,
he doesn't have the doubt.*

That's what he possesses.

—**Ron Wolf** on Brett Favre after
Favre's first game-winning TD pass

CHAPTER 2
COMEBACKS

✯✯✯✯✯✯✯✯✯✯

*Anybody can throw a touchdown
in the second quarter.*

*But when you're late in the game, you're
down, and that defense is coming at you,
what are you going to do?*

That's when I like playing the game.

—Brett Favre

Brett Favre fans took pride in knowing that no matter how little time was left in a game, or how far the Packers had to go to score, Favre could pull out a win.

"Some people squeeze and get a little tighter," Packers Head Coach Mike Holmgren said about players and pressure. "Brett's one of those guys who relaxes and says, 'Give me the ball.'"

Last-minute comebacks brought out the best in Favre and—tough as he was—even brought him to tears at least once.

Favre's most impressive string of comebacks launched the 1999 season. It was his first in Green Bay without his mentor, Holmgren, who had left for the Seattle Seahawks. He also faced the challenge of playing with a right thumb injury that would have stopped other quarterbacks.

In the season opener against the Oakland Raiders, safety LeRoy Butler recalled Favre's throwing hand "looked like somebody ran over it with a car."

The pain got so bad (and the Raiders already had made three interceptions) that Favre considered benching himself. But with the Packers trailing 24–21, and less than two minutes and no timeouts left, Favre capped an 82-yard drive with his fourth touchdown pass. The Packers won, 28–24.

Tears streamed from the 29-year-old's eyes as he spoke to reporters after the game.

"I'm so drained right now," he said. "I just can't believe I played. I could hardly feel the ball, but we won the game."

Through 2006, Favre led the Packers to 36 wins when they were tied or trailing in the fourth quarter.

And in 9-of-36 comebacks, Favre pulled out the win with a touchdown pass, or a TD run of his own, during the final two minutes. The first was Kitrick Taylor's score.

The other eight game-winning touchdowns were just as thrilling.

1. TAMPA BAY BUCCANEERS AT LAMBEAU FIELD, NOVEMBER 28, 1993

The "most boring close game in Lambeau Field history," according to one veteran reporter, ended with drama.

With 7:33 remaining against the then-lowly Tampa Bay Buccaneers, Green Bay got the ball on its own 25-yard line, trailing 10–6. The Packers had been kept out of the end zone and had more punts than points. Then Favre led the team on a 15-play drive that lasted more than six minutes, completing key third-down passes to tight end Ed West and wide receiver Mark Clayton.

On second-and-goal at the 3, when Favre rolled right and couldn't find an open receiver, he tried to run for the score. Bucs safety Barney Bussey drilled his helmet into Favre's left thigh, sending him cartwheeling.

"Next thing I knew I was doing a 360 in the air, and I knew I wasn't in the end zone," Favre said. "I had to call time out. I couldn't have went if we had just lined up and played right there, so I called time out. But once I went to the sidelines, I bent down and took a rest, and I knew I could come back."

On the next play, Favre rolled right again. His first two throwing options were covered. But then wide receiver Sterling Sharpe streaked across the back of the end zone, and Favre hit him for the score with 1:16 to play. The Packers held on to win 13–10.

"I had my head down, and I was hurting," Favre said about the timeout before throwing the 2-yard TD. "But in that situation I couldn't let the guys down. We'd come too far for me to stop right there."

2. AT DETROIT LIONS, WILD CARD GAME, JANUARY 8, 1994

The Packers and Lions had played 127 times over 64 years, but this was their first post-season matchup. The Lions had good reason to be confident.

Green Bay hadn't won a playoff game in a non-strike season since Super Bowl II, 27 years earlier. And in the '93 season finale, the Lions had beaten the Packers 30–20 in Detroit, with Favre throwing four interceptions. The Wild Card game would be played in Detroit, too, just six days later.

The game was close all the way. In the second half, Packers rookie safety George Teague scored on a 101-yard interception return, setting an NFL post-season record. But in the fourth quarter, with just 55 seconds left, the Lions led 24–21.

That's when Favre made the play of the year.

Scrambling away from a heavy rush, Favre ran backward and to his left, then threw across his body—60 yards in the air—to Sharpe, who was racing down the right sideline.

"I figured, 'What the heck?'" Favre said. "'I'll give it the big heave-ho.'"

The pass found Sharpe alone in the end zone for a 40-yard touchdown, his third of the game, giving the Packers a 28–24 win.

"I lost my helmet, my ear pads. I started hyperventilating," Favre said. "I was looking for someone to kiss."

3. ATLANTA FALCONS, FINAL GAME AT COUNTY STADIUM, DECEMBER 18, 1994

For 62 seasons, the Packers split their home games between Green Bay and Milwaukee. The final forty-two Milwaukee games were played at County Stadium, onetime home of baseball's Milwaukee Braves and Milwaukee Brewers. The tradition ended in 1994, when the Packers honored their Brew City fans with one last exciting finish.

The Packers hosted the Atlanta Falcons, the team with the growing regret for having given up on Favre two years earlier. With 1:58 remaining, Atlanta led 17–14. The Packers had the ball on their own 33-yard line, but without Sharpe, their star receiver, who had been injured in the second quarter. Favre completed 6-of-8 passes, landing his team at the Falcons' 9-yard line with 14 seconds left. The Packers had no timeouts, which meant that running a play was risky: If they didn't score, there might not be enough time to kick a field

Favre crashing into the end zone on a 9-yard scoring run with 14 seconds left in the game. The play lifted the Packers to a 21–17 win against the Atlanta Falcons on December 18, 1994, in the Packers' final game at County Stadium in Milwaukee.

goal to put the game into overtime.

On the next play, Favre went back to pass, scrambled right—and then decided to run. A touchdown would win the game—and keep the Packers' playoff hopes alive. Favre eluded one defender, then dived under another, crossing the goal line for the winning score.

"I probably couldn't have wrote it any better. It was either get in, or we lose it," he said.

"I kept telling everybody somebody was going to make a play. I just didn't think it would be me."

The Packers' 21–17 victory was a dramatic farewell to Milwaukee, where they finished with a 107–63–1 record. They clinched a playoff spot with a victory the next week.

When Holmgren left the field, he climbed a pile of snow near the first-base dugout, pumped his fists into the air and blew kisses to the crowd of 54,885. "Thank you,

Milwaukee! Thank you!" he hollered over and over.

The win also signaled a turning point in Favre's development as a leader.

"He came into the huddle, calmed everybody down and just took control," said tight end Mark Chmura. "That's the first time I really saw him like that."

Defensive end Reggie White thought Favre's play presaged a much bigger Packers' victory.

"If he keeps playing like he's playing," White said, "he's going to take us where we want to go."

A little more than two years later, Favre would lead the Packers to a victory in Super Bowl XXXI.

4. OAKLAND RAIDERS AT LAMBEAU FIELD, SEPTEMBER 12, 1999

The game that left Favre in tears ended with a drive that turned three little-known players into heroes.

With Oakland leading 24–21, Favre moved the Packers downfield, mostly with passes

Favre celebrating the game-winning touchdown over the Atlanta Falcons with tight-end Mark Chmura and receiver Robert Brooks.

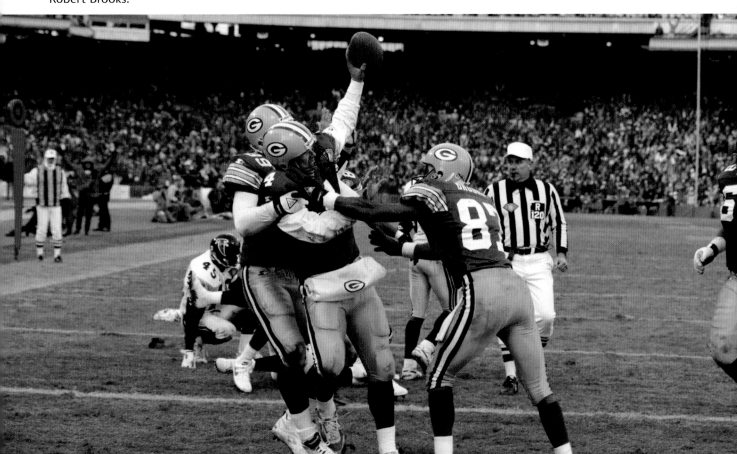

over the middle. The team reached the Raiders' 20-yard line with 20 seconds to go. That's when Favre found wide receiver Corey Bradford on a fade route down the right sideline. He beat cornerback Charles Woodson, perhaps the NFL's best cover corner at the time, for a 19-yard gain to the 1.

With 15 seconds left, the Packers sent in three tight ends—Mark Chmura, Tyrone Davis, and Jeff Thomason—and lined them up wide, with Davis and Thomason to the right. When the ball was snapped, Davis broke toward Thomason, picking off Oakland safety Anthony Newman. Favre hit Thomason for the 1-yard score and the 28–24 win.

Some writers ripped Oakland for losing in Ray Rhodes' debut as the Packers' head coach. But they missed the point. *San Francisco Examiner* reporter Gwen Knapp, for example, groaned about the fact that two of the last three passes in Green Bay's winning drive were caught by converted track stars—Bradford and wide receiver Bill Schroeder; both of them had played only one year of college ball. Knapp also lamented how the winning TD was caught by Thomason, a third-string tight end who had caught a total of 28 passes in six seasons before that game. It was Thomason's only play from scrimmage the whole day.

The point, though, was not that the Raiders let themselves be beaten by two track stars and a third-stringer—it was that Favre could bring out the best in every one of his teammates.

The rally took a ruinous toll on Favre, who completed 28-of-47 passes for 333 yards on the day. He collapsed from exhaustion on the play before the winning touchdown and, after the score, had to be helped to the bench. At the post-game news conference, he buried his face in his hands and lightly sobbed. After a half-minute of silence, he got up and left the room, too weak to speak, apologizing to reporters on his way out.

"What he showed us is that he cares. He really cares," running back Dorsey Levens said of Favre's emotional breakdown. "He's not in it for the money, he's not in it for the fame, he really wants to win football games. If the guys on this team can see that he's the highest-paid player on the team and he still does it for love, then they know they need to get their priorities straight."

5. MINNESOTA VIKINGS AT LAMBEAU FIELD, SEPTEMBER 26, 1999

After the thrilling win over the Raiders to start the '99 season, the Packers lost to the Lions in Detroit. Now they were back home, bracing for the Minnesota Vikings. For some Packer fans, Minnesota had become Green Bay's arch-rival, given how poorly the Chicago Bears were playing against the Pack.

In the victory over Oakland, Favre had started the winning drive trailing by three points with 1:52 remaining and 82 yards to go for a touchdown. It was nearly the same against Minnesota, although the Packers trailed by four—20–16—with 1:51 left and 77 yards to go.

Favre had dried his tears and was wearing his war face again.

"Favre had the ball in his hands, about two minutes to go on the clock, and the undivided attention of the Minnesota Vikings," Mike Freeman wrote in *The New York Times.* "There was a sense of dread that he was about to do something to ruin their day. They were right."

In the game-winning drive, Favre made "sublime quarterbacking seem almost a matter of routine," *Milwaukee Journal Sentinel* reporter Bob McGinn wrote. "No other quarterback can spin like a top, set up hurriedly with the rush closing in, and find (Corey) Bradford between three defenders with an absolute bullet for 22 yards. That started the 77-yard winning march."

The drive looked like it might stall at the Vikings' 23-yard line. Green Bay faced fourth-and-one, with 20 seconds and no timeouts remaining; most of the Packers looked helpless and confused at the line of scrimmage. But Favre was calm. He looked like he was browsing through a library, one reporter wrote; no, perusing a menu, wrote another.

He was so cool, in fact, he never called a play.

"I don't think I even said 'hut,'" Favre said, describing how exhausted he was. "I just told everybody to line up. If the ball was snapped, I knew they'd do something. This game's not that complicated."

Favre started with a pump-fake to Schroeder, who was running down the right side, before throwing to Bradford in the end zone for a 23-yard score and a 23–20 win. On the day, Favre completed 24-of-39 passes for 304 yards.

With the win, Favre boosted his home record to 50–6—which, at the time, was the best such mark in NFL history. Writers measured him against the greatest quarterbacks of all time.

"This was Unitas and Layne and Graham and Elway and Staubach at their best, taking command of a game when all looked lost," the *Chicago Tribune's* Don Pierson wrote.

After the score, Favre ran across the field pumping his fists and was met at the sideline by linebacker Brian Williams, who hugged him as they fell into a heap. Moments later, Favre was seen stretched out on the bench, taking oxygen.

He downplayed his performance after the game.

"I'm too tired to cry today," Favre said in the post-game news conference.

"Hey, I'm just a big kid out there playing."

Favre wasn't sure whether he witnessed Bradford's TD catch, but he knew his pass was perfect.

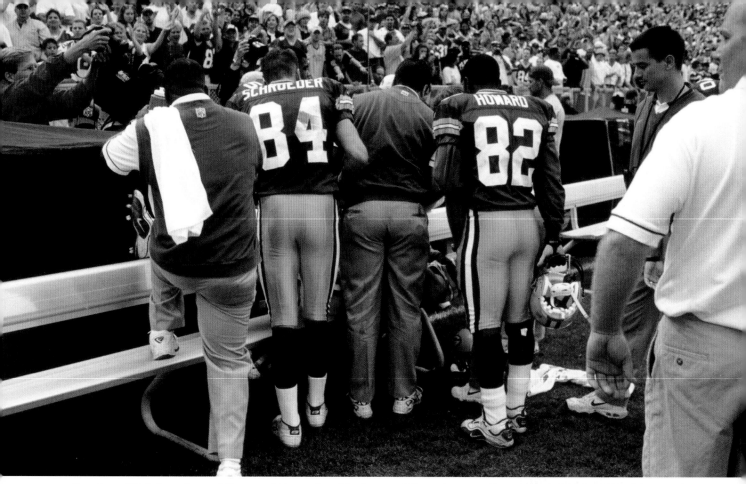

Receivers Bill Schroeder and Desmond Howard and Packers staff hovering over Favre, who is barely visibly lying on the bench. Favre collapsed from exhaustion near the end of a game against the Minnesota Vikings on September 26, 1999. With the Packers trailing 20–16 and less than two minutes to go in the game, Favre led the team on a 77-yard scoring drive for a 23–20 win.

"I kept my head down then and listened to the crowd," Favre said. "When they started cheering, I said, 'We got it. Either that, or they're very drunk.'"

Bradford sounded like Kitrick Taylor.

"I was in a dream, and I figured sometime I would wake up," he said. "When I did, it was in the end zone."

Apparently this was a team of dreamers.

"Those touchdown passes, I've dreamed about them a million times since I was a kid," Favre said.

"Of course, Corey Bradford wasn't in them."

6. TAMPA BAY BUCCANEERS AT LAMBEAU FIELD, OCTOBER 10, 1999

Three days after the Vikings win, Favre revealed he had aggravated the thumb injury that nearly benched him in the season opener against Oakland and also had played through the flu. Following a bye week, he would be tested by the Tampa Bay Buccaneers, who grabbed a 23–19 lead with about two minutes to go.

Celebrating his thirtieth birthday and the Packers' retirement of Reggie White's number, Favre raced his team 73 yards in 40 seconds. He punctuated the winning drive with a 21-yard touchdown pass to wide receiver Antonio Freeman. Seeing the Buccaneers coming on an all-out blitz, Favre had exchanged a look with Freeman, who made the catch with 1:05 to play despite pass interference by cornerback Ronde Barber.

The Bucs were in shock.

"We stepped on their throats, we had them in the casket, we were ready to put the nail in…" said defensive tackle Warren Sapp. "I would have bet my life we would have stopped them on that last drive."

"We got Favre'd," was how Tampa quarterback Trent Dilfer put it. "I don't know what else you can say. He's the absolute best there is."

Favre re-injured his thumb again but played through it, leaving Tampa 0–9 at Lambeau during the 1990s.

"The young man is what I would say is the ultimate warrior," Rhodes said. "You'd have to look in the guy's eyes and see the emotion, the tears and everything that goes on with him."

Favre called the dramatic wins over Oakland, Minnesota, and Tampa the most draining of his career. But he kept his humor.

"I'm just doing what they pay me to do," he said.

"Hell of a way to make a living, I can tell you that."

7. MINNESOTA VIKINGS AT LAMBEAU FIELD, NOVEMBER 6, 2000

Favre never threw two touchdowns in a game that were more jaw-dropping than the two in this one. One was the "improbable bobble." It beat the Minnesota Vikings. In overtime. On Monday Night Football.

What could be better?

The game was tight all night at cold, wet, and windy Lambeau Field. In the third quarter, the Packers tied the score at 20 after running back Ahman Green followed Allen

Rossum's 90-yard kickoff return with a 2-yard scoring run.

Green also had scored the Packers' first touchdown in one of Favre's playground-like moves. While being taken down to the ground, Favre tossed the ball underhand to Green for a 5-yard score.

"We practice that one all the time," Favre joked.

There was no way to practice Favre's other TD pass.

The game had gone into overtime—still tied at 20—after the Vikings failed to get off a 32-yard field goal attempt with 7 seconds left in regulation. Punter Mitch Berger mishandled the snap. Then, instead of falling on the ball and calling a timeout to give his team another chance—it was first down—he made a pathetic attempt at a pass. The ball was intercepted by cornerback Tyrone Williams.

Berger later called himself an idiot.

(*I didn't feel bad for him. But I did for the guys sitting next to me who actually went home before the Vikings tried the kick! You never leave a game like that early—those are the kinds of games where memories are made.*)

In overtime, the Packers won the coin flip and sloshed from their own 18-yard line through a driving rain to the Vikings' 43. Center Frank Winters asked for and got a dry ball. Favre, facing a blitz on third-and-four, launched a pass toward Freeman.

ABC-TV announcer Al Michaels called the pass incomplete. Even now, it isn't easy to follow what happened. Vikings cornerback Cris Dishman had "tipped the pass off his right hand and then his left arm," according to Packers.com. "Freeman, who was sliding after making a head-first dive for the throw, corralled it as he remained on the ground at the 15-yard line, with the ball caroming off his shoulder and facemask before being controlled by the receiver's extended right hand. As the veteran receiver watched Dishman run past him, Freeman alertly jumped to his feet and raced to the end zone."

The Vikings, said Jim Souhan of the *Minneapolis Star Tribune*, were left "looking around as if for a pickpocket."

No one could believe Freeman had caught the pass, so it seemed impossible that suddenly he was up again and running, carrying the ball into the end zone.

"I'm looking around," Favre said, "and (Freeman) gets up running, and I'm going, 'What is he doing?' I didn't even know he had the ball. So I run down there and jump on him, and during all the mayhem, I just kind of whispered to him, 'Hey, did you catch it?'"

Maybe it's best to leave a little mystery in the story.

Ron Jaworski of ESPN called the catch "one of the greatest game-ending plays in NFL history," and NFL Films President Steve Sabol agreed.

8. AT JACKSONVILLE JAGUARS, DECEMBER 3, 2001

Most opponents knew never to brazenly challenge Favre—or he would do to them what he did to the Jacksonville Jaguars.

Late in the third quarter of this Monday Night Football matchup, the Jaguars stripped Favre and returned the fumble 60 yards for a touchdown, taking a 21–7 lead. Then first-year defensive tackle Marcus Stroud mouthed off to Favre.

Favre—who earlier in the game had thrown the first left-handed touchdown pass of his career, a little shovel pass to Green—responded by throwing a 43-yard TD to Schroeder. Later, he hit Freeman with a 29-yard bullet to set up the tying touchdown pass to tight end Bubba Franks.

Finally, with 1:30 remaining and the ball on the Jaguars' 6-yard line, Favre rolled left on second-and-goal. Rather than throw to Franks, who was covered in the end zone, or to fullback William Henderson, who was short of the end zone, he ran. Defensive end Tony Brackens, who had stripped Favre for the Jags' defensive score, gave chase. But Favre beat him around the corner and slipped past another tackler into the end zone for a 28–21 win.

Favre always rose to the challenge at crunch time. He might have wished there weren't so many of them, though.

"Everybody talks about how much fun it looks like I'm having," he once said. "We'll be down by three points with two minutes to go and we get the ball back, and people say it's my time, that this is what I live for. Even my teammates will say it. They expect me to pull it out. Well, that's tough.

"Sometimes I want to say, 'Hey, let's have a blowout every once in a while.'"

✫✫✫✫✫✫✫✫✫

Just when you think he's run out of heroics, he does something you've never seen before.

—Mike Wahle
Packers guard
on Brett Favre

Jacksonville Jaguars defensive tackle Tony Brackens forcing a Favre fumble that was returned for a touchdown, and Favre responding with his own 6-yard TD late in the game on December 3, 2001. The Jaguars' TD gave them a 21–7 lead late in the third quarter. After the fumble, Jaguars rookie defensive end Marcus Stroud mouthed off to Favre. Favre responded by leading the Packers to a 28–21 come-from-behind win, beating Brackens around the corner on his game-winning run.

BRETT FAVRE'S 36 COMEBACK WINS

Victories in which Favre rallied the Packers to victory after they were tied or losing in the fourth quarter.

KEY: Number/ Date/ Opponent/ Final Score/ Score at Start of Drive/ Quarter/ Timeouts to Use/ Timeouts Used/ Clock at First Play from Scrimmage/ Clock at End of Drive/ Scorer/ Yards/ Scoring Play/ Drive Plays/ Yards/ Time of Drive

#	Date	Opponent	Final Score	Score at Start	Qtr	TO to Use	TO Used	Clock First	Clock End	Scorer	Yards	Scoring Play	Drive Plays	Yards	Time
1.	09/20/92	Cincinnati	24–23	17–23	4	2	0	1:07	0:13		35	pass to Taylor	5	92	0:54
2.	11/15/92	Philadelphia	27–24	24–24	4	2	1	0:43	0:00	Jacke	41	field goal	2	0	0:43
	11/15/92	Philadelphia	27–24	21–24	4	2	0	5:02	1:31	Jacke	31	field goal	8	60	3:31
3.	11/29/92	Tampa Bay	19–14	12–14	4	3	0	2:12(3Q)	10:09		9	pass to Harris	15	69	7:03
4.	11/14/93	at N. Orleans	19–17	16–17	4	0	0	1:37	0:03	Jacke	36	field goal	10	56	1:
5.	11/21/93	Detroit	26–17	16–17	4	2	1	12:29	9:03	Jacke	34	field goal	7	42	3:26
6.	11/28/93	Tampa Bay	13–10	6–10	4	3	0	7:33	1:16		2	pass to Sharpe	15	75	6:17
7.	01/08/94*	at Detroit	28–24	21–24	4	3	1	2:26	0:55		40	pass to Sharpe	5	71	1:31
8.	10/09/94	L.A. Rams	24–17	17–17	4	3	0	0:27(3Q)	12:06	Bennett	1	run	6	40	3:21
9.	12/18/94	Atlanta	21–17	14–17	4	1	1	1:58	0:14	Favre	9	run	10	67	1:44
10.	11/12/95	Chicago	35–28	28–28	4	3	0	13:05	9:17		16	pass to Bennett	8	69	3:48
11.	10/14/96	San Francisco	23–20	20–20	OT	2	0	13:25	11:19	Jacke	53	field goal	7	21	2:06
	10/14/96	San Francisco	23–20	17–20	4	2	1	1:42	0:08	Jacke	31	field goal	10	69	1:42
12.	11/01/98	San Francisco	36–22	22–22	4	3	0	11:13	11:04		62	pass to Freeman	1	62	0:09
	11/01/98	San Francisco	36–22	19–22	4	3	0	1:09(3Q)	13:14	Longwell	45	field goal	7	36	2:55
13.	12/27/98	at Chicago	13–13	16–13	4	3	1	2:29(3Q)	9:49	Longwell	18	field goal	12	74	7:40
14.	09/12/99	Oakland	28–24	21–24	4	0	0	1:51	0:11		1	pass to Thomason	11	82	1:40
15.	09/26/99	Minnesota	23–20	16–20	4	2	2	1:51	0:12		23	pass to Bradford	7	77	1:44
16.	10/10/99	Tampa Bay	26–23	19–23	4	3	1	1:40	1:05		21	pass to Freeman	6	73	0:40
17.	09/17/00	Philadelphia	6–3	3–3	4	2	2	5:20	0:03	Longwell	38	field goal	12	60	5:17
18.	10/15/00	San Francisco	31–28	28–28	4	2	2	5:20	0:54	Longwell	35	field goal	9	44	4:36
19.	11/06/00	Minnesota	26–20	20–20	OT	2	0	14:50	11:21		43	pass to Freeman	7	82	3:39
20.	12/24/00	Tampa Bay	17–14	14–14	OT	2	0	14:47	8:29	Longwell	22	field goal	10	58	6:31
21.	12/03/01	at Jacksonville	28–21	21–21	4	3	0	2:03	1:30	Favre	6	run	4	56	0:33
22.	12/30/01	Minnesota	24–13	10–13	4	3	0	9:58	6:28	Green	4	run	7	79	3:35
23.	01/13/02*	San Francisco	25–15	15–15	4	3	0	11:48	7:02	Longwell	45	field goal	10	49	4:58
24.	09/08/02	Atlanta	37–34	34–34	OT	2	0	9:30	5:15	Longwell	34	field goal	7	44	4:15
25.	09/29/02	Carolina	17–14	10–14	4	2	0	6:29	4:10		22	pass to Driver	4	65	2:19
26.	12/08/02	Minnesota	26–22	20–22	4	2	1	4:32	1:06	Fisher	14	run	9	85	3:26
27.	11/02/03	at Minnesota	30–27	20–20	4	3	1	2:20(3Q)	13:14		12	pass to Walker	9	73	4:12
28.	11/16/03	at Tampa Bay	20–13	13–13	4	3	0	3:36(3Q)	9:00	Green	1	run	17	98	9:42
29.	12/14/03	at San Diego	38–21	17–21	4	3	0	12:02	11:18		40	pass to Ferguson	2	42	0:52
30.	01/04/04*	Seattle	33–27	13–20	4	3	0	1:51(3Q)	10:01	Green	1	run	12	60	6:56
	01/04/04*	Seattle	33–27	20–20	4	3	0	9:30	2:44	Green	1	run	12	51	6:46
31.	11/14/04	Minnesota	34–31	31–31	4	2	2	1:11	0:00	Longwell	33	field goal	5	39	1:20
32.	11/21/04	at Houston	16–13	13–13	4	2	2	2:00	0:00	Longwell	46	field goal	8	41	2:00
	11/21/04	at Houston	16–13	10–13	4	2	0	11:08	7:55	Longwell	39	field goal	7	40	3:13
	11/21/04	at Houston	16–13	3–13	4	3	0	14:53	12:28		24	pass to Driver	7	81	2:25
33.	12/12/04	Detroit	16–13	13–13	4	2	1	3:27	0:02	Longwell	23	field goal	10	37	3:25
	12/12/04	Detroit	16–13	10–13	4	2	0	11:45	10:46	Longwell	28	field goal	5	44	0:59
34.	12/24/04	at Minnesota	34–31	31–31	4	2	2	1:35	0:00	Longwell	29	field goal	11	76	1:35
	12/24/04	at Minnesota	34–31	24–31	4	3	1	8:18	3:34		3	pass to Driver	13	80	4:44
35.	12/11/05	Detroit	16–13	13–13	OT	3	0	15:00	9:43	Longwell	28	field goal	10	56	5:17
36.	12/21/06	Minnesota	9–7	6–7	4	1	1	1:14	0:04	Rayner	44	field goal	7	41	3:13

CHAPTER 3
COLD

✶✶✶✶✶✶✶✶✶✶✶

*They pay me a lot of money
to play in those conditions.*

—Brett Favre on
playing in the cold

For a boy from balmy Rotten Bayou, Brett Favre sure was at home in the cold. In his first thirty-five home games when the temperature at kickoff was 34 degrees or lower at kickoff, Favre went 35–0.

Through 2006, Favre was 42–6—an 87.5 percent success rate.

Along the way, he made many teams wail for their warm blankies.

NOVEMBER 23, 1997
PACKERS 45, DALLAS COWBOYS 17

The deer hunters' blaze orange may have clashed with the gold "Title Towels" on this day at Lambeau. But when it's four degrees below zero, Packer fans throw fashion to the wind.

This was a day made for cold-cocking the Cowboys.

Favre and his former Atlanta Falcons teammate, Deion Sanders, chatting at a Packers-Dallas Cowboys game on November 23, 1997. Sanders intercepted a Brett Favre pass and returned it 50 yards for a touchdown, but the Packers won at a frigid Lambeau Field, 45–17.

Dallas hoped to extend its eight-game winning streak—including three playoff victories—over the Pack. At halftime, each team had had the ball fifteen minutes, and the score was tied at 10.

But in the second half, Green Bay scored on each of its four possessions, steamrolling Dallas with drives of 69, 73, 61, and 88 yards. For good measure, rookie safety Darren Sharper returned a fumble recovery for a touchdown.

Big D's defense had come into the game ranked second in the league. It left having given up more points than any Dallas squad had in twelve seasons.

The offense didn't have much, either.

"It was a pretty good whippin' the second half," quarterback Troy Aikman said.

"The last time I got beat like this was by my father," added receiver Michael Irvin, "(and) my father's been dead for quite a while."

Irvin had dropped two balls he would have caught in warmer weather and Hall of Fame running back Emmitt Smith fumbled two handoffs.

Dallas deserved a deep freeze. The last seven of the previous eight matchups with Green Bay had been played in Texas—the final one serving as strong motivation for the Packers. In that game, with his team leading 18–6 with 20 seconds to go, Dallas Head Coach Barry Switzer called a timeout so that Chris Boniol could tie an NFL record by kicking his seventh field goal of the day.

On the day of retribution, much of the punishment was inflicted by Packer running back Dorsey Levens, who posted a franchise-record 190 yards on 33 carries. Favre even audibled out of passing plays to give Levens the ball.

"I knew we had them when they left the field two minutes early in warm-ups because of the cold," Levens said.

The pounding by the Packers took its toll. Dallas linebacker Randall Godfrey got flagged for two cheap shots, including a roundhouse to Favre's helmet; and, after the game, Godfrey had the gall to call Green Bay the dirtiest team he'd faced.

"We're just a bunch of dirty bandits," joked Packers tackle Ross Verba.

Favre threw for all four of the offense's touchdowns, but he did blow it on one play. Deion Sanders made an interception and returned it 50 yards for a TD. Even the supremely self-centered one, however, gave Favre his due.

"He's absolutely unbelievable," Sanders said. "He is truly the most valuable player in this league, because without Brett Favre, the Green Bay Packers are not the Green Bay Packers."

DECEMBER 26, 1993
PACKERS 28, LOS ANGELES RAIDERS 0

The temperature at kickoff was zero degrees.

"You had to retrain your thought process," Favre recalled. "Your face was frozen. You couldn't speak in the huddle."

I can still feel how cold my toes were that day. And sitting along the railing just above the visitors' tunnel, I could see that the beach-boyish L.A. team just wanted to go home.

"I just watched the clock," said Raider running back Rickey Dixon, who later became a Packer. "I said to myself, 'Somehow, some way, I got to get out of here.'"

While the Raiders longed for their locker room, the Packers made it a historic day:

- Favre's touchdown pass to Sterling Sharpe made Sharpe the first player in NFL history to post back-to-back seasons with 100 or more catches.

Favre trying to stay warm on December 26, 1993, when the temperature at kickoff was zero degrees. The Packers beat the Los Angeles Raiders 28–0.

- Safety LeRoy Butler forced a fumble that defensive end Reggie White recovered and lateraled back to Butler. Butler scored and jumped into the stands, creating the Lambeau Leap.

- The Packers clinched their first playoff berth under Head Coach Mike Holmgren and their first since 1982.

DECEMBER 31, 1995
NFC WILD CARD GAME: PACKERS 27, ATLANTA FALCONS 20

Favre awoke to freshly fallen snow, which told him the Atlanta Falcons were in big trouble for the NFC Wild Card Game. The temperature reached 30 degrees by kickoff, but Lambeau Field offered fog, as well as flurries, to contend with.

It was a throwback kind of day, wrote Bob Ford of the *Philadelphia Inquirer,* "missing only John Facenda in a voice-over role."

The Falcons talked big, having defeated the world champion San Francisco 49ers the previous week to make the playoffs. The cockiness showed in the first quarter, when Eric Metcalf caught a Jeff George pass for a 65-yard touchdown—and then Metcalf teased as though he would make a Lambeau Leap.

"It was the last time the game would seem very humorous for Atlanta," Ford wrote.

In the first half, Favre completed passes to nine receivers. When the Falcons closed to within 27–17 early in the fourth quarter, he drove his team 70 yards, hitting Levens with an 18-yard pass for a touchdown.

"That kind of drove the stake in their heart," Favre said.

The next day, the NFL announced Favre had won the first of what would be an unprecedented three consecutive Most Valuable Player awards.

DECEMBER 11, 1994
PACKERS 40, CHICAGO BEARS 3

The temperature was 15 degrees with a wind chill of 6 degrees—the coldest game between the two teams in 18 seasons. The Bears took a 3–0 lead, then got flattened with 40 unanswered points.

Bears defensive lineman Alonzo Spellman, who had been dumb enough to guarantee a victory at Lambeau, claimed to have no regrets.

"The bottom line is that the media here took what I said and I guess cut some of the words out. It got Brett Favre kind of fired up," Spellman said.

No doubt. The Packers gained 516 yards—including Favre's 250 yards passing—dwarfing the Bears' total of 176.

"On a normal day, I can throw with the best of them," Favre said. "On a day like this, I am the best one."

★★★★★★★★★★

Hey, Brett Favre is from Mississippi— he'll be just as cold.

—Carolina Panthers cornerback **Eric Davis** before the Packers beat Carolina 37–20 in the 1996 NFC Championship Game

MORE HOME-IN-THE-COLD MOMENTS

- Favre passed for 319 yards in Green Bay's overtime playoff win over the Seattle Seahawks on January 4, 2004. Seattle won the coin flip to start overtime, but then quarterback Matt Hasselbeck made a doomed proclamation: "We want the ball. We're going to score." He promptly threw an interception to cornerback Al Harris, who returned it for a touchdown, giving the Packers a 33–27 win. "It hurts," said Mike Holmgren, who had become the Seahawks' head coach. "I'll be honest with you, I'm dying inside."

- On December 1, 2002, Favre entered the game against the Chicago Bears having thrown seven interceptions in the previous two games, both losses. He had been sick all week, even straining to hear during practice. The Bears led 14–3 in the second quarter, but then Green Bay ripped off 27 unanswered points to win its first division title in five years.

- Against the Minnesota Vikings on December 30, 2001, Favre went 5-for-5 on a fourth-quarter drive that gave the Packers the lead for good en route to a 24–13 win. Earlier, he had leveled safety Orlando Thomas with a devastating block, clearing the way for a 31-yard touchdown run by wide receiver Donald Driver. "That's the only way I know how to play," Favre said. "Give it up for the team."

Packers defensive end Reggie White getting emotional after Favre gave him an NFC Champions hat on January 12, 1997 in "Ice Bowl II."

ICE BOWL II

The week before the biggest—and coldest—game he ever played in at Lambeau Field, Brett Favre was throwing up.

Reggie White was having bad dreams.

The game, on January 12, 1997, was for the NFC Championship—the first championship game at Lambeau since the famed Ice Bowl of 30 years earlier.

And yet, some Packers seemed unfazed.

Two days before the game, wide receiver Andre Rison was sipping Tanqueray gin, smoking an El Producto cigar and waiting for a limousine to take him to the Milwaukee Bucks game against the world champion Chicago Bulls. "Yeah, this is our time!" he screamed. "We're gonna blow up; we've gotta lock down. We've gotta do like the Bulls, like the Yankees—the champions of the world!"

On game day at Lambeau, where someone had put an ice sculpture of the Lombardi trophy in the parking lot, Packers Bob Kuberski, Mike Flanagan, and Marco Rivera—all of whom were inactive for the game—walked onto the field coatless, with big grins on their faces, wearing "NFC Champions" T-shirts. Quite a show of confidence, given the minus-17 wind chill, the coldest at Lambeau since the Ice Bowl.

Favre and White hadn't slept all week. White complained about one bad dream he had about the Panthers game, saying, "One or two plays and it was over. And I'm trying to figure out, did we win or what?"

Favre suffered, too.

"You can't get away from the game in this town," he said. "You can't even watch *Seinfeld* on television anymore, because they've pushed it out of the way for more Packers coverage. You can't go out to eat, because you spend all your time talking to people about the NFC Championship game. It's great, but it got to the point where I couldn't sleep. My wife and I spent all night tossing and turning with our butterflies. We didn't know who was going to throw up first."

For Favre, the anxiety seemed to carry over to the field. One day in practice, he threw a couple of interceptions, infuriating Head Coach Mike Holmgren. "You're the league MVP, and you're looking like a rookie out there," Holmgren snarled. Favre started the game disastrously, throwing an interception that linebacker Sam Mills returned to the 2-yard line, setting up an easy Carolina touchdown. Favre tied the game at 7 with a 29-yard touchdown pass to running back Dorsey Levens, who gained 205 total yards on the day. But then Favre fumbled without being touched, enabling Carolina to kick a field goal and retake the lead, 10–7.

"I wasn't so much worried as I was embarrassed," said Favre. "I thought I was done with those plays."

The chill, however, set in by the second quarter for Carolina—which, in 32 games as a franchise, had played in only one game with the temperature below 35 degrees.

The Packers stormed back with 10 points in the final minute of the first half to take a 17–10 lead. Favre ended a 15-play, 71-yard drive with a 6-yard TD pass to wide receiver Antonio Freeman, and then the Packers kicked a field goal after an interception by cornerback Tyrone Williams.

All told, Green Bay scored on five straight possessions and amassed a team-record 479 yards of total offense. Favre completed 19-of-29 passes for 292 yards and two touchdowns as Green Bay won going away, 37–20.

One of Favre's completions combined superior athletic ability, toughness and childlike play.

The Packers were leading 17–10 early in the third quarter, facing third-and-seven at the Carolina 32-yard line. With Panthers Kevin Greene and Mark Thomas dragging him down from behind, Favre, while falling forward, made a two-handed, basketball-style pass to Levens for an 8-yard gain and a first down. The play kept alive a drive that ended in a 32-yard Chris Jacke field goal.

Favre, who didn't see the completion after being knocked down by Greene, said, "I got back up after the play, and he looked at me and said, 'Wow!'"

When Favre jogged to the sidelines near the end of the game, he was met by White. Michael Silver of *Sports Illustrated* wrote:

> As 60,790 fans shook Lambeau Field to its icy core, Favre received a wool cap, a 1996 NFC Champions hat and a bear hug from defensive end Reggie White, whose smile could have melted the most frozen tundra. "Congratulations, you deserve this," Favre whispered into White's ear, and the big man lost it. Steam rising from his head and tears running down his cheeks, the 35-year-old, 300-pound White turned into a bundle of mush.

Even Holmgren became choked up after the game as he walked to every player's locker, saying, "Thank you! Thank you!"

White, a minister, viewed the victory as proof that God had led him to choose Green Bay when he signed with the Packers as a free agent four years earlier. "Whether you want to believe it or not, we've gotten here because the Lord has blessed us," he said. Sitting next to White, Favre interjected, "I believe, Reggie, I believe."

After leaving the locker room, Favre lingered awhile, according to an account from Bill Pennington of the *Bergen* (N.J.) *Record.* Tailgating Packers fans near Favre, "their faces lit by the barbecue blazes, saw their quarterback and let loose an ovation that seemed to grow as it bounced off the frozen, snow-covered asphalt," he wrote. "Favre then paused to sign autographs, to pose for pictures, to answer football questions. He did everything but grab a brat from the grill."

Now there was a player who appreciated his fans.

GOLD IN THE COLD
Brett Favre won his first 35 games at home when the
temperature at kickoff was 34 degrees or below.
Overall, including playoff games, he was 40–5 through 2006.

**Date/ Opponent/ Temperature/ Passing Attempts/ Completions/ Yards/
Percentage/ TDs/ Interceptions/ QB Rating/ Game Score/ Won-Lost**

1992
Date	Opponent	Temp	Att	Comp	Yards	Pct	TD	Int	Rating	Score	W/L
Nov. 15	Philadelphia	28°	33	23	275	69.7	2	2	89.8	27–24	W
Nov. 29	Tampa Bay	32°	41	26	223	63.4	1	0	85.7	19–14	W
Dec. 6	Detroit*	26°	19	15	214	78.9	3	0	153.2	38–10	W
Dec. 20	St. Louis	8°	23	14	188	60.9	2	1	97.7	28–13	W

1993
Date	Opponent	Temp	Att	Comp	Yards	Pct	TD	Int	Rating	Score	W/L
Nov. 28	Tampa Bay	29°	36	23	159	63.9	1	0	83.0	13–10	W
Dec. 26	L.A. Raiders	0°-sunny	28	14	90	50.0	0	0	83.9	28–0	W

1994
Date	Opponent	Temp	Att	Comp	Yards	Pct	TD	Int	Rating	Score	W/L
Dec. 11	Chicago	15°-sunny	31	9	250	61.3	3	1	105.6	40–3	W
Dec. 18	Atlanta*	33°-sunny	44	29	321	65.9	2	1	93.1	21–17	W
**Dec. 31	Detroit	33°-p. cldy	38	23	262	60.5	0	0	81.3	6–12	W

1995
Date	Opponent	Temp	Att	Comp	Yards	Pct	TD	Int	Rating	Score	W/L
Nov. 12	Chicago	22°-cloudy	33	25	336	75.8	5	0	147.2	35–28	W
Nov. 26	Tampa Bay	34°-cloudy	24	16	267	66.7	3	0	143.6	35–13	W
Dec. 3	Cincinnati	32°-p. cldy	43	31	339	72.1	3	1	108.6	24–10	W
Dec. 24	Pittsburgh	24°-cloudy	32	23	301	71.9	2	0	122.0	24–19	W
**Dec. 31	Atlanta	30°-lt. fog	35	24	199	68.6	3	0	111.5	37–20	W

1996
Date	Opponent	Temp	Att	Comp	Yards	Pct	TD	Int	Rating	Score	W/L
Dec. 1	Chicago	29°-flurries	27	19	231	70.4	1	0	108.7	28–17	W
Dec. 8	Denver	31°-cloudy	38	20	280	52.6	4	2	89.8	41–6	W
Dec. 22	Minnesota	31°-overcast	23	15	202	65.2	3	0	132.6	38–10	W
**Jan. 4	San Francisco	34°-rain	15	11	79	73.3	1	0	107.4	35–14	W
**Jan. 12	Carolina	3°-sunny	29	19	292	65.5	2	1	107.3	30–13	W

1997
Date	Opponent	Temp	Att	Comp	Yards	Pct	TD	Int	Rating	Score	W/L
Nov. 23	Dallas	22°-pt. cldy	35	22	203	62.9	4	1	104.8	45–17	W
Dec. 20	Buffalo	31°-cloudy	18	12	156	66.7	2	0	130.8	31–21	W
**Jan. 4	Tampa Bay	28°-cloudy	28	15	190	53.6	1	2	57.1	21–7	W

1998

Dec. 20	Tennessee	29°-snow	22	14	253	63.6	3	0	142.6	30–22	W

1999

Jan. 2	Arizona	32°-lt. rain	34	21	311	61.8	2	1	99.0	49–24	W

2000

Nov. 19	Indianapolis	27°-lt. snow	36	23	301	63.9	2	1	97.1	26–24	W
Dec. 10	Detroit	25°-pt. cldy	36	15	208	41.7	1	1	58.6	26–13	W
***Dec. 24	Tampa Bay	15°-sunny	42	20	196	47.6	0	2	41.4	17–14	W

2001

Dec. 9	Chicago	33°-sunny	27	15	207	55.6	1	1	77.2	17–7	W
Dec. 23	Cleveland	24°-lt. snow	28	18	139	62.1	3	0	112.1	30–7	W
Dec. 30	Minnesota	19°-pt. cldy	29	18	169	62.1	0	0	78.1	24–13	W
**Jan. 13	San Francisco	28°-sunny	29	22	269	75.9	2	1	112.6	25–15	W

2002

Nov. 4	Miami	30°-clear	25	16	187	64.0	1	1	83.2	24–10	W
Dec. 1	Chicago	23°-cloudy	42	24	221	57.1	2	1	77.6	30–20	W
Dec. 8	Minnesota	11°-clear	32	22	214	68.6	2	1	95.1	26–22	W
Dec. 22	Buffalo	27°-pt. sun	33	15	114	45.5	1	2	39.2	10–0	W
**Jan. 4	Atlanta	31°-snow	42	20	247	47.6	1	2	54.4	27–7	L

2003

**Jan. 4	Seattle	20°-overcast	38	26	319	68.4	1	0	102.9	33–27***W	

2004

Nov. 29	St. Louis	28°-pt. cldy	27	18	215	66.7	3	0	127.9	45–17	W
Dec. 12	Detroit	33°-flurries	36	19	188	52.8	1	0	77.1	16–13	W
Dec. 19	Jacksonville	12°-clear	44	30	367	68.2	2	3	80.4	28–25	L
**Jan. 9	Minnesota	26°-cloudy	33	22	216	66.7	1	4	55.4	31–17	L

2005

Dec. 11	Detroit	14°	31	21	170	67.7	0	1		16–13	W
Dec. 25	Chicago	34°	51	30	317	58.8	0	4		24–17	L
Jan. 1	Seattle	34°	37	21	259	56.7	1	1	76.3	23–17	W

2006

Dec. 3	New York Jets	19°-flurries	47	24	214	51.1	1	2	53	38–10	L

*Game played in Milwaukee
**Playoff game
***Overtime
Source: packers.com

CHAPTER 4
MVP

✶✶✶✶✶✶✶✶✶✶

My personality, even though I don't say many things, is that I believe I can win the MVP.

I believe I can be the quarterback in the Super Bowl and in the Hall of Fame one day.

I believe all those things.

I think if I didn't, I wouldn't be sitting here today.

—Brett Favre after winning his first Most Valuable Player award

It's easy to get caught up in the statistics Brett Favre put up in his back-to-back-to-back Most Valuable Player seasons.

But if you did, you'd forget how much fun we had watching him make plays:

Favre pinballing around in the pocket, scrambling toward one sideline, half-circling back toward the other—then arching a pass across his body and into the arms of a receiver on the opposite side of the field.

Throwing off his back foot, underhand, side-arm, left-handed.

Scanning the field for what seems like forever, spotting an opening the size of a football, firing a pass that seems sure to be intercepted—but instead goes for a touchdown.

Favre never conceded an inch, never doubted his arm, never gave up on a play.

"He just will not let the team lose," said Packers Head Coach Mike Holmgren.

In winning three *consecutive* MVPs—no one else in NFL history has won three, period—Favre posted otherworldly numbers. During the 1995, '96 and '97 seasons, he threw for 12,000 yards and 112 touchdowns; he completed an average of 60 percent of his passes; he even ran for six scores.

Along the way, the Packers won 77 percent of their games (37–11) and captured the Central Division title each year. After the 1996 season, they went to the Super Bowl for the first time in 29 years and won it. And they returned to the Super Bowl the next season, only to be denied by John Elway and the Denver Broncos.

Favre's trademark skill was making plays—improvising and innovating when all seemed lost.

Favre conferring with General Manager Ron Wolf and Head Coach Mike Holmgren after a game during the 1996 season. Wolf hired Holmgren in January 1992 and traded for Favre a month later.

Having a cannon for a right arm helped, of course. Linemen said they could hear Favre's passes. Announcers insisted there were vapor trails behind them. And receivers broke fingers trying to catch them.

Favre "could throw a football through a car wash without it getting wet," wrote Bill Lyons of the *Philadelphia Inquirer*.

There were hundreds of those car-wash throws. In a '95 game against the Cincinnati Bengals, the Packers were trailing 10–3 with 6 seconds left in the first half "when Favre gets desperate at the Bengal 13-yard line," according to this account by Bill Plaschke of the *Los Angeles Times*:

> No receivers are open. A field goal will allow the Bengals to maintain momentum. Favre needs a touchdown. But how to get it? Then he sees Mark Ingram standing in the end zone, sandwiched by Bengal safeties Bracey Walker and Darryl Williams. None of them are expecting the ball because no right-minded quarterback would ever try to thread that sort of . . . The ball flies into the crowd, so quick and hard and accurate that the safeties' outstretched hands can't get it and the surprised Ingram can't miss it. It hits him in the belly. The Packers tie the game and never trail again. "A miracle," Packer coach Mike Holmgren says.

Favre was much more, however, than a man with a gun. His determination is what carried him. You don't make the kind of plays he did without being supremely confident that you can pull them off.

That fire was stoked long before Favre was anybody in the NFL, as *Milwaukee Journal Sentinel* reporter Bob McGinn could attest. McGinn described one of Favre's first sit-down interviews shortly after he arrived in Green Bay in 1992. The 22-year-old, second-year player was asked to consider some of the greats of the game: John Elway, Dan Marino, Troy Aikman.

"I can do anything they can do," Favre told his stunned interviewer. "There's nobody in the league that I look at in awe. I just haven't proven it yet."

In less than five months, Favre proved himself right into the Pro Bowl, alongside Aikman. And within three years, he was on his way to his first MVP award.

"There are some quarterbacks that can outrun me, probably out-throw me, ones that are more accurate," Favre said late in the '95 season. "But why aren't you hearing about them? What separates me from some other guy who's the same size as me, same speed, same arm and everything? It's the fire inside, the emotion. I love to play the game."

Repeat MVP winners

*Players who won the Associated Press vote for
the NFL's Most Valuable Player more than once*

Three times
Brett Favre, Green Bay Packers   **1995, 1996, 1997***

Two times
Jim Brown, Cleveland Browns   1957, 1965
Johnny Unitas, Baltimore Colts   1964, 1967
Joe Montana, San Francisco 49ers   1989, 1990
Steve Young, San Francisco 49ers   1992, 1994
Kurt Warner, St. Louis Rams   1999, 2001
Peyton Manning, Indianapolis Colts   2003**, 2004

Shared with Barry Sanders, Detroit Lions
**Shared with Steve McNair, Tennessee Titans*
Source: packers.com, NFL.com

SUR-PASSING PERFORMANCES

Brett Favre's passing statistics during his three consecutive MVP seasons

**Year/ Attempts/ Completions/ Yards/ Completion %/ Yards per Attempt/
TDs/ Interceptions/ Longest-Pass yards/ Times Sacked, Yards Lost/ Passer Rating**

1995/ 570/ 359/ *4,413/ 63.0/ 7.7/ *38/ 13/ *99T/ 33/ 217/ 99.5
1996/ 543/ 325/ 3,899/ 59.9/ 7.2/ *39/ 13/ 80T/ 40/ 241/ 95.8
1997/ 513/ 304/ 3,867/ 59.3/ 7.5/ *35/ 16/ 74/ 25/ 176/ 92.6

*Led NFL
T=Touchdown
Source: packers.com

Favre's passion showed in plays that were never diagrammed—the kind that could make your heart race, or nearly stop.

One of the best plays gashed the hated Dallas Cowboys during the '95 season. The Packers were on the Cowboys' 21-yard line, down two touchdowns late in the fourth quarter, when Favre called a pass play. Plaschke, the *L.A. Times* guy, loved this one, too:

> He looks. Nothing there. He scrambles, looks some more. There are still no holes in the Cowboy zone, so he begins to run down the left side. When he has reached the 14-yard line, he is caught by Dallas safety Brock Marion. Inexplicably, Favre pump fakes, even though he is *six yards beyond* the line of scrimmage. Stranger still, Marion *falls for the fake,* momentarily hesitating. Favre sprints into the end zone.

In game 12 against the Tampa Bay Buccaneers that season, Favre showed his ability to make plays for huge yardage. The offense used just 14 plays to score four touchdowns; three came on Favre passes, and each of those was on a second or third read, including a 54-yard strike to wide receiver Robert Brooks. And yet, the most dazzling play was a quick hit to Brooks after Favre made a series of whirling dervish moves. Plaschke one more time:

> Favre runs a play in which he is supposed to roll right before throwing. He rolls, but there is nobody open on the right side. So he stops and runs left. Still nobody open. By then, the defensive backs figure he will run and begin pressing. Huge mistake. Out of the corner of his eye, Favre sees Brooks standing in the middle of the end zone, far from his assigned route, just hanging around until he hears a whistle or witnesses an incredible feat, as all of Favre's receivers learn to do. And he gets one. Favre stops running left, spins, and throws the ball blindly over his left shoulder. Right to Brooks for the touchdown. On the sideline, Holmgren chants the familiar litany of, "No, no, no, no . . . Yes!"
>
> Favre's best touchdown pass this season covered all of three yards.

"I can't even believe it happened; that was a miraculous thing," Holmgren said. "Now I'm hoping that if (Favre) is on like that. . . this might be something special this year."

The team became truly special the next season, during the 1996 run to the Super Bowl. Favre showed it in a road win over the St. Louis Rams in game 12. This time, a breakdown by Bernie Miklasz of the *St. Louis Post-Dispatch:*

There was a telling play early in the fourth quarter, when Favre threw the knockout punch on a 5-yard touchdown pass to Dorsey Levens. Favre was trapped, hemmed in by the Rams' pass rush. At least three Rams had a chance to nab him, but Favre wouldn't give in. Favre kept moving, bouncing, looking, running. On a play that was all heart and guts, Favre at that moment simply wanted to succeed more than the Rams did. He wouldn't be denied. He just wouldn't lose this one-play battle. Favre outfought the Rams, and then he dropped them with the TD pass to Levens. The Packers sealed it, 24–9.

"That was the most unbelievable play I've ever seen on the field of play," said Rams defensive back Todd Lyght. "He broke four tackles on one play."

Favre achieved his goal of winning a Super Bowl that season, but his resolve burned just as strongly during the '97 season. Even when he wasn't at his best, he made the difference. In game three, it was Favre's mobility that lifted Green Bay to a 23–18 win over Dan Marino and the Miami Dolphins—the Packers' first win over the Fish in nine tries. Denied the long ball by a persistent pass rush, Favre stayed calm, looked through his progression of receivers, and smoothly led scoring drives of 72, 82, 78, and 83 yards. He kept the drives alive by slipping out of sacks and scrambling to complete passes. Miami defensive line coach Cary Godette estimated that against a less mobile quarterback, his team would have made at least three sacks instead of one, plus a half-dozen more pressures on passing plays. "I just missed him four or five times," said rookie defensive end Jason Taylor, an expression of disgust on his face.

Favre could even win games on reputation alone. In game seven of '97, Chicago Bears Head Coach Dave Wannstedt so feared Favre's ability to make plays with the game on the line that he went for a two-point conversion rather than an extra point with 1:54 remaining. An extra point would have tied the game. But after Erik Kramer overthrew his target on the conversion attempt, the Packers ran out the clock for a 24–23 win, dropping the Bears to 0–7, the worst start in their 78-year history. "I don't want to give them that chance," Wannstedt said of his decision to try and win the game rather than tie it. "You have to have a lot of respect for their 2-minute drill."

Favre's ability to operate under pressure confounded and dispirited one team after another. Fans could see what *Packer Plus* writer Jeff Potrykus put into words after game 14 of the '97 season, when the Packers flattened the Buccaneers on their home turf, 17–6.

How many other quarterbacks can move deftly up in the pocket to avoid pressure, locate an open receiver streaking down the middle of the field, and then fire a bullet more than 40 yards for a touchdown? Favre did just that when he hit Robert Brooks for a 43-yard touchdown to put the Packers ahead for good with 4 minutes 46 seconds left in the first quarter.

How many other quarterbacks can scramble away from more pressure, pumping the ball with every other step, and then, just before reaching the line of scrimmage and with a defender wrapped around his legs, find an open receiver near the goal line for another score? Favre did just that in the third quarter when he scrambled as close to the line of scrimmage as the rules allow and, with defensive tackle Warren Sapp trying to drag him down from behind, found Dorsey Levens open in the middle at the 1-yard line.

A humbled Sapp could only shake his head after the game: "He steps up in the pocket, people crawling all over him. He finds a dude on the 1-yard line. Touchdown."

The next week, Green Bay beat the Carolina Panthers 31–10 for its third straight road win, something the team hadn't achieved in 34 years. Highlights included Favre's 58-yard touchdown pass to wide receiver Antonio Freeman. According to the *Journal Sentinel's* McGinn, it took 1.55 seconds for the pass to travel 37 yards from the right hash mark to the right sideline. "Favre's ability to throw touchdowns probably is the key factor why all these road victories suddenly seem so routine," McGinn wrote. "With a run-of-the-mill quarterback, touchdowns become field goals and routs become dogfights."

Winning doesn't come from talent alone, however, and the Packers wouldn't have become champions without Favre having grown as a leader. He developed a poise that made his teammates believe he could take on any challenge.

In a game against the Detroit Lions during the '95 season, the Packers squandered a 20–0 halftime lead and had to rely on Favre to save them. With the game on the line in the fourth quarter and the Packers leading by just six points, Favre drove the team 66 yards for a Chris Jacke field goal to boost the lead to 30–21. He had converted a crucial third-and-thirteen by withstanding a blitz and launching a 35-yard pass to wide receiver Charles Jordan, who was the third option on the play. Later in the quarter, Favre ate up time on the clock with another drive, which was highlighted by a 33-yard pass to tight end Mark Chmura on third-and-two. Chmura had gotten behind linebacker Chris Spielman, whom Favre had memorably stiff-armed earlier in the game.

Favre's play had reached a pinnacle. As Kent Youngblood of the *Wisconsin State Journal* observed, not only had Favre tied an NFL record by throwing two or more touchdowns in 12 consecutive games, but in the past five games, he had thrown fewer interceptions (three) than in any other five-game span of his career. Moreover, even without injured star receiver Sterling Sharpe, the Packers were 4–2, their best start in 17 years.

Throughout his MVP run, when Favre wasn't single-handedly carrying the team, he showed leadership by influencing his teammates.

Near the Buccaneers' goal line in a 1995 game, Favre went back to pass and saw both of his elite tight ends open. Chmura, his best friend, was in the clear, but Favre threw the touchdown to Keith Jackson, who had felt underused since coming to the team in mid-season. "I want to get him involved. We need all the weapons we can get," Favre said.

In the '96 season, Favre showed how he could get his teammates to step up. With starting receivers Brooks and Freeman out with injuries, Favre took on Don Majkowski and the Detroit Lions with split ends Terry Mickens and Anthony Morgan, neither of whom had played the previous season; and with flankers Don Beebe, who had been cut by the expansion Carolina Panthers, and rookie Derrick Mayes, who had three NFL receptions. Undaunted, Favre went 24-of-35 for 281 yards and four touchdowns. (Majkowski, meanwhile, got sacked five times by his former teammates.) The 28–13 win was the twelfth straight at Lambeau, breaking the team record.

Favre even showed leadership by bonding with players who weren't easy to like.

Wide receiver Andre Rison showed up in mid-season 1996, about a year after a feud between Rison and Favre had been re-ignited. When Rison first became available as a free agent, Favre had said he was glad the Packers didn't sign him because he had been bad for morale when the two played for the Atlanta Falcons. Rison responded by calling Favre a hillbilly. (Asked if the comment hurt his feelings, Favre replied with a laugh, saying, "No, I am a hillbilly.")

But, feud or no, Rison led the team with five receptions in his first game as a Packer, the 24–9 win over St. Louis. Favre wouldn't let any carping compromise the team.

"Watching Favre embrace Rison as the third quarter ended showed just what type of leader Favre is," the *Journal Sentinel's* McGinn wrote of that game.

"He means everything to this team."

★★★★★★★★★★

He's not only a teammate.
This is Brett Favre.
He is the Green Bay Packers.
He's us, and we're him.

—Packers center **Mike Flanagan**

Tight end Tyrone Davis and wide receiver Terry Mickens celebrating a touchdown in Green Bay's 31–21 win over the Buffalo Bills on December 20, 1997, to close out the 1997 season. Davis scored on a fumble recovery and on a Favre TD pass in the game. Favre threw 35 touchdowns in '97, leading the league for the third straight year.

MVPs, SEASON BY SEASON

1995 SEASON

Brett Favre knew the expectations of him would be high in 1995, his fourth season in Green Bay.

Head Coach Mike Holmgren had told a kickoff luncheon he was putting the ball in Favre's hands and that everything rested on his shoulders.

"I almost choked on my chicken cordon bleu," Favre said.

Favre had some sense that his upside was very high. Assistant Coach Steve Mariucci had been telling him he would be the NFL's Most Valuable Player one day.

"I'm like, 'Yeah, OK, whatever,'" Favre would say. "'Let's get the meeting over with and get the hell out of here.'"

Favre admitted later, however, that he took Mariucci's comments to heart, and his play showed it. The Packers rocketed to an 8–1 start in '95, with Favre throwing 24 touchdowns and just seven interceptions.

By game 15, the MVP award seemed a lock. Favre led a 34–23 disassembling of the Saints in New Orleans, completing 21-of-30 passes for 308 yards and four touchdowns. "He was just in total command of this game," said an emotional Mariucci, who was leaving Green Bay to become head coach at the University of California.

For his part, Favre said he should be considered for MVP, "but I don't vote on it."

The election was a landslide. Favre won votes from 69-of-88 sports writers and broadcasters; 49ers receiver Jerry Rice was second with 10 votes. In becoming the fourth Packer to win the award, and the first since Bart Starr in 1966, Favre had set an NFL record with 4,413 passing yards and an NFC record with 38 touchdown passes. He had seven three-touchdown games and three four-touchdown games. And inside the 20, Favre was a killer: a 60 percent completion rate with 31 TDs and only three interceptions.

More importantly, Favre led the Packers to their first NFC Central title in 23 years. Then he directed the team to playoff victories over the Atlanta Falcons and the San Francisco 49ers. The 27–17 triumph in San Francisco, where the Packers were 10-point underdogs, was especially sweet.

The game featured the league's two most recent MVPs—Favre and 49ers quarterback Steve Young, who had won it in '92 and '94. Aided by an aggressive defense, Favre easily outperformed Young, completing fifteen of his first seventeen passes and finishing 21-of-28 for 299 yards and two touchdowns. Favre's 75 percent completion rate set a team record. The win denied the 49ers a trip to the NFC Championship Game for the first time in five years.

Sitting in the stands at that game, it was clear to me that Favre and Green Bay had turned the corner. Even the dejected 49ers fans jumped aboard, telling me and the other Cheeseheads that they were backing the Pack and that we had to beat Dallas. That didn't come to pass. But there were no doubts that with Favre in charge, winning a world championship was merely a matter of time.

1996 SEASON

Favre had to overcome many obstacles to repeat as MVP.

In May, Favre disclosed that he had a Vicodin addiction. After a forty-six-day inpatient stay at the Menninger Clinic, proclaimed he would win a Super Bowl.

Once again, here was a guy fans could rally behind. Clearly, Favre had been in denial for some time about his addiction. But when he confronted it, he went public and redoubled his commitment to win.

The other obstacles were a result of injuries: offensive lineman Ken Ruettgers, a 12-year-veteran, retired at mid-season; leading receiver Robert Brooks was lost for the season October 14; wide-out Antonio Freeman missed four games and tight end Mark Chmura missed three.

It all seemed to bring out the best in Favre. He threw 39 touchdown passes, up one from 1995, leading the league for the second straight year. He had five four-TD games—one of them against the Denver Broncos, who had the league's top-rated defense.

Among the more memorable games was a tilt against the Philadelphia Eagles in the first *Monday Night Football* game at Lambeau Field in 10 years. At first, the added excitement seemed to bring out the youthful Favre. He "air-mailed his first five passes to peanut vendors, surprised Eagle defenders, officials, and just about anyone not in a Packer uniform," *Packer Plus* reporter Brad Zimanek wrote. "I told him to settle down," said Mark Chmura. "He wanted me to go up to him and smack him in the head and get it over with."

The maturing Favre re-emerged, however, and by halftime he had thrown for 222 yards, including two touchdown passes to Brooks. "Favre is unconscious right now," easily the best quarterback in the league, Detroit Lions scout Rick Spielman said at intermission. "No one comes close to him."

Coming off a 34–3 demolition of the Tampa Bay Buccaneers in the season opener, the Packers' 39–13 shellacking of the Eagles led *Chicago Tribune* writer Don Pierson to correctly predict that Green Bay would win the Super Bowl going away: "Season's over. Packers win," Pierson wrote after week two. "In case you missed it, the fledgling NFL race came to a dramatic and sudden halt Monday night in Green Bay. The Packers not only pummeled the Philadelphia Eagles, they beat every other team that tuned in. Everybody's playing for second."

Favre agreed that the Packers were just warming up. "I can get better, I really can; we all can," he said. "It's kind of a scary thought."

The next week, the Packers waxed the San Diego Chargers 42–10. The contest was so one-sided that, with two minutes to go, according to Austin Murphy of *Sports Illustrated,* Favre could be seen on the sideline "yukking it up with defensive end Reggie White and eating Gummi Bears out of a paper cup."

In the playoffs, Green Bay dispatched the San Francisco 49ers 35–14 before defeating the Carolina Panthers in Ice Bowl II (see Chapter 3—Cold) and the New England Patriots in the Super Bowl (see Chapter 5—Super Bowl). Favre went 44-of-71 (62 percent) during the playoffs for 617 yards and five touchdowns, with only one interception.

1997 SEASON

Favre had to scratch and claw—sometimes literally—to capture his third straight MVP award, which he shared with Detroit Lions running back Barry Sanders.

Favre logged his second career five-touchdown game in game three, a 38–32 defeat of the Minnesota Vikings that featured its share of chippy play. Frustrated when they couldn't sack Favre, the Vikings frequently hit him after the play, causing Favre to do his share of pushing, shoving, and trash talking.

"It's hard to explain what it's like to play a football game," he said. "All you care about is kicking the guy's tail across from you. I kind of had that mentality. I wanted to kick their tail, too."

Fortunately, Favre kept his cool as the Packers saw their 31–7 halftime lead shrink to 31–22 early in the third quarter. After Green Bay got the ball on its 19-yard line, Vikings defensive tackle John Randle stalked the line, screaming at the Pack, "I'm coming! We're gonna bring it! You'll never stop us!" But nine plays and 81 yards later, Favre completed his fifth pass of the drive to Chmura for a 2-yard touchdown, sealing the game. "Their guys are kicking him, pushing him, spitting on him, and he's still throwing touchdowns," Green Bay safety LeRoy Butler said of Favre. "Without him we'd be lost."

Favre's performance peaked as the season neared its end. One example: game 14 against the Buccaneers, which Bob McGinn of the *Milwaukee Journal Sentinel* called "the most ballyhooed pro football game" played in Tampa since 1979 when the Bucs advanced to the NFC Championship Game. At halftime, the Packers led by just a point, 7–6, but they so dominated the second half that, in the end, Packer fans seemed to take over what was left of the franchise-record crowd of 73,000-plus. The Packers won 17–6 and clinched their third straight division title.

"The big bully came in and beat us in our own backyard," defensive lineman Warren Sapp said.

"It's really embarrassing, to be quite honest with you," quarterback Trent Dilfer added. "I don't know whose fault it is, and I'm not casting the blame on anybody, but it's embarrassing. They're celebrating the championship at our place, and it's loud and obnoxious. It's like they're playing at home."

Favre had completed 25-of-33 passes for 280 yards and two touchdowns, becoming the first player in NFL history to throw for 30 TDs in four consecutive seasons.

"Favre is 28 years old, in his seventh season and at the absolute pinnacle of his game," McGinn wrote. "With his teammates on offense bumbling through the first half it remained for Favre to hold the fort until they shaped up…Whether it was eluding three sacks when he was dead to rights, zipping swing passes on the money or dancing away from pressure and making plays with his arm and feet, Favre was the master of the situation."

"Even Holmgren 'couldn't find room for improvement.' I don't know what more we could ask of Brett Favre," he said.

"The answer is nothing," McGinn wrote.

In the season finale, the Lambeau Field crowd was hushed when Favre was leveled on the game's second play by 280-pound defensive lineman Phil Hansen of the Buffalo Bills. "It scared me more than anything. I couldn't breathe there for a few minutes," Favre said.

Favre not only rose from the turf but, on second-and-four late in the second quarter, bounced off a hit by Hansen and eluded two other tacklers while rolling left to complete an 8-yard pass to Chmura. Chmura looked dumbfounded as Favre headed his way before firing a bullet for the first down. His teammates were left inspired: another jaw-dropping play in a game that had no playoff implications.

"He's going to get himself killed one of these days," said guard Aaron Taylor, "but that's why he's the best in the league."

By this point, Favre already knew he had been voted co-MVP, but Holmgren made sure it didn't go to his head.

"He came up to me at one point during the game, and he put his arm around me, which he never does. I'm always thinking someone's going to dump water on me when he does that," Holmgren said. "And he said, 'Listen, I've got something to tell you. I got it again.' I said, 'That is so great, I'm proud of you.' Then I said, 'I've got something to tell you. I knew three days ago.'"

Five years later, in 2002, Favre nearly won a fourth MVP. Oakland Raiders quarterback Rich Gannon took the honors. Favre finished second, just four votes behind.

✱✱✱✱✱✱✱✱✱✱

Favre in August 1993, preparing to start his second season as a Green Bay Packer.

Favre stretching on the practice field during training camp in August 1993.

Head Coach Mike Holmgren mentoring Favre after a game in 1993.

Favre sharing a laugh in January 1994 with trainer Pepper Burruss. Favre was always known for being a prankster in the locker room and having as much fun as possible on the field.

Favre pumping iron in January 1997.

Favre autographing his jersey in 1997.

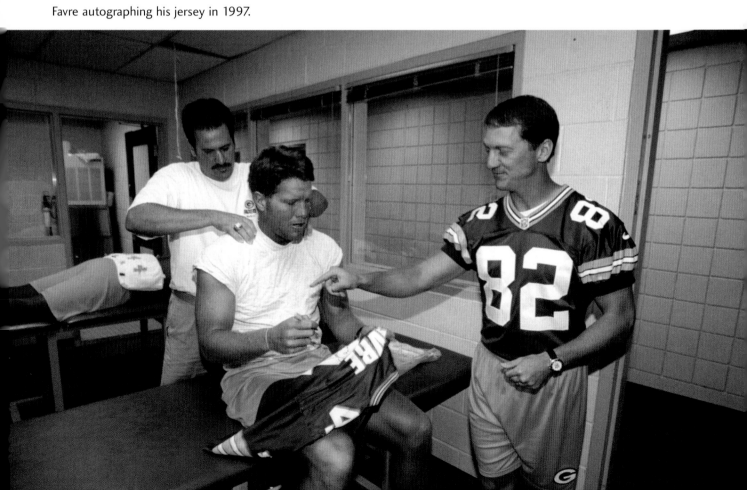

Favre and his father, Irvin Favre, in January 1998. Irv Favre died at 58 after suffering a heart attack near his Mississippi home in 2003.

Favre in 1998 with San Francisco 49ers quarterback Steve Young (left) and 49ers head coach Steve Mariucci, who was an assistant at Green Bay during Favre's early years with the Packers.

New England Patriots quarterback Drew Bledsoe with Favre on July 31, 1997, before the Packers beat the Patriots 7–3 in a preseason game played six months after the Packers beat the Patriots in Super Bowl XXXI.

Favre signing an autograph for a flight attendant on a plane in August 1998.

Favre surveying the field during the 1999 season.

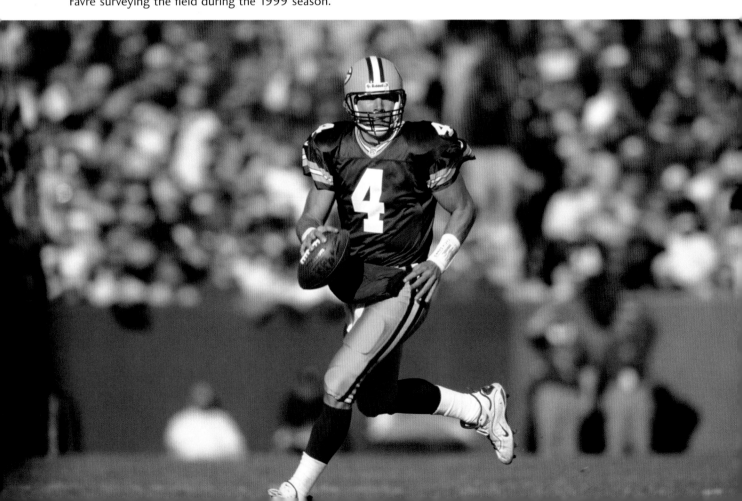

Favre with his thoughts in October 1999.

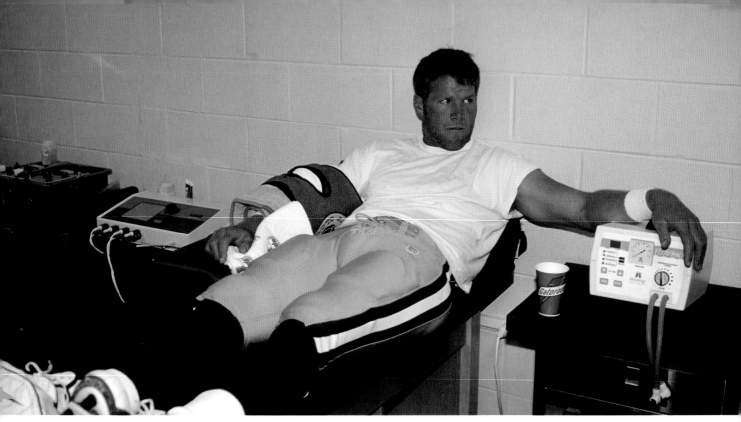

Favre getting an arm treatment in the locker room in 2002.

Favre and Tampa Bay Buccaneers defensive lineman Warren Sapp on October 7, 2001. Favre enjoyed jawing with his opponents, especially Sapp.

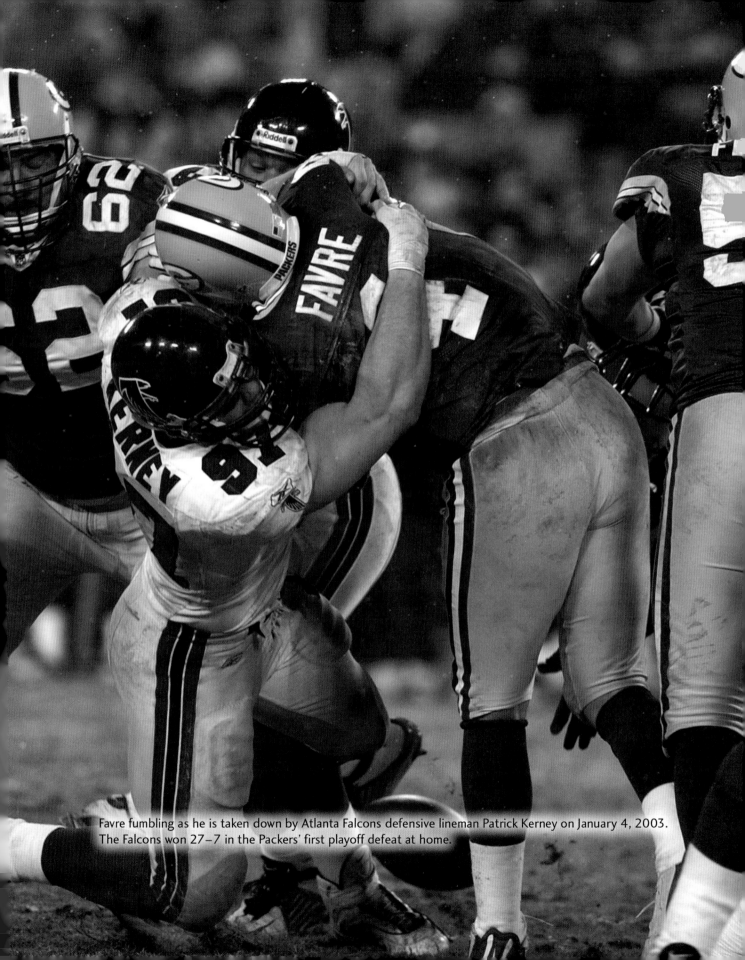

Favre fumbling as he is taken down by Atlanta Falcons defensive lineman Patrick Kerney on January 4, 2003. The Falcons won 27–7 in the Packers' first playoff defeat at home.

Favre pounding a fist into the turf in the 2004 season opener against the Carolina Panthers. Favre made mistakes but never let them keep him from playing to win. The Packers won the *Monday Night Football* matchup 24–14.

Favre and running back Ahman Green celebrate a victory over the Denver Broncos on December 28, 2003.

Favre showing a mellower side on the sidelines.

Right: Favre's locker at Lambeau.

Below: Assistant trainer Kurt Fielding writing a prediction about the Packers' game against the Seattle Seahawks on January 1, 2006. Fielding's predictions were a game ritual. For this game, Fielding correctly predicted a Packer win.

Favre played under Head Coach Mike Sherman for six years. "If you polled Americans on what player they would most like to be, I believe Brett Favre would be a near-unanimous choice," Sherman said.

From the time Favre became the Packers' starting quarterback, early in the 1992 season, through the 2005 season, the Chicago Bears, Minnesota Vikings, and Detroit Lions had a total of 45 starting quarterbacks. Green Bay used one—and he always played all out. "I'm playing to win, as though each play is my last play," Favre said.

Favre showing anguish during a 28–25 loss to the Jacksonville Jaguars on December 19, 2004. "There haven't been too many games I've lost that a tear hasn't come out of my eyes because it means that much to me. I take things hard," Favre said.

Favre showing some of the fire that he kept burning throughout his career. In this game, the Packers defeated the New Orleans Saints 52–3 on October 9, 2005, the day before Favre's 36th birthday.

Favre celebrating with Donald Lee during the Saints game. Leaping into a receiver's arms was a trademark of Favre's.

Favre in the locker room with teammates after the December 21, 2006, game against the Minnesota Vikings. At the time, it was thought that game could be Favre's last at Lambeau Field.

Favre with wife, Deanna, and daughters Breleigh (left) and Brittany (right). Deanna Favre had requested the picture before the December 21, 2006, game against the Minnesota Vikings.

Favre in the tunnel at Lambeau Field waiting his turn to run onto the field before his 200th consecutive start.

Favre waving to his family after the Packers defeated the St. Louis Rams 45–17 on November 29, 2004, on *Monday Night Football*. The waves were a ritual for Favre.

Favre with Packers president Bob Harlan during a ceremony honoring the retiring CEO at the December 21, 2006, game against the Minnesota Vikings.

Favre never lost his intensity on the field, as he shows at the line of scrimmage in this game on October 30, 2005, against the Cincinnati Bengals.

The 2005 season, when Green Bay finished 4–12, was especially hard on Favre and on all Packer fans. The Bears beat the Packers twice, including this game on December 4.

Favre in a lighter moment with Indianapolis Colts quarterback Peyton Manning on September 26, 2004. Manning was the only quarterback active during Favre's career who seemed to have even a remote chance of beating Favre's consecutive-games-started streak for quarterbacks.

Favre entering the locker room at Lambeau Field after his final game of the 2005 season. Many had wondered whether the 23–17 win over the Seattle Seahawks on New Year's Day 2006 would be Favre's last game. Favre had said at the start of the 2001 season: "I can't say I can't wait for it to be over, but when it's over, I'll be fine. Because I've put as much into it as I possibly can, and I've gotten as much out of it as anybody."

CHAPTER 5
SUPER BOWL

****

You know, I'm going to beat this thing.

I'm going to win a Super Bowl.

*And all I can tell people
if they don't believe me is:*

Just bet against me.

—Brett Favre, May 1996, after
treatment for Vicodin addiction

Brett Favre had prepared his whole life for Super Bowl XXXI. But that didn't mean he couldn't use some advice from his savvy—and nutty—backup quarterback, Jim McMahon.

Eleven years earlier, in the days leading up to Super Bowl XX, McMahon had made news almost daily: tweaking the NFL by wearing banned headbands, including one bearing the name of Commissioner Pete Rozelle; exposing his buttocks to a helicopter hovering over a practice session; and saying nasty things (a false accusation, it turned out) about New Orleans women.

"He's kind of filled me in on how to moon a helicopter, how to talk about the women down there," Favre said. "I know exactly what not to do, talking to him."

Had Super Bowl XXXI been played during Favre's partying days, he might have made as many headlines as McMahon did. But several months before the 1996 season, Favre suffered a seizure in front of his then-girlfriend and their 7-year-old daughter during routine treatment for an ankle injury. "Mom, is he going to die?" a terrified Brittany Favre had asked. The seizure seemed related to an addiction Favre had to the painkiller Vicodin. He finally admitted the problem, checked himself into the Menninger Clinic in Kansas for six weeks of rehabilitation and emerged to famously predict that he would win a Super Bowl.

All of which meant Favre wouldn't be out causing trouble while preparing for the New England Patriots in New Orleans—the same team McMahon's Chicago Bears had annihilated in the same place eleven years earlier. But Favre did follow McMahon's lead to ease his nerves shortly before kickoff.

Favre and Head Coach Mike Holmgren speaking at a news conference in May 1996. Favre announced that he was entering inpatient treatment for an addiction to the painkiller Vicodin.

"McMahon starts throwing footballs at the nameplates on the lockers, knocking guys' names off," Favre recalled in *Playboy* magazine. "Pretty soon we're all doing it. Me, McMahon and a bunch of other guys. Balls are flying all over the room. Holmgren comes in and says, 'What the hell is this?'"

You could picture the scene—too bad it didn't make the pre-game show on television.

Favre was plenty loose coming out of the locker room; the Packers scored on their second play from scrimmage.

New England had gotten the ball first but quickly punted, leaving the Packers to start their first drive near mid-field. On second-and-nine from their own 46, Favre was supposed to make a short pass to tight end Keith Jackson. Instead, he audibled to "74 Razor," a post pattern for wide receiver Andre Rison. In the face of six blitzing defenders, Favre hit Rison at the Pats' 21-yard line, and Rison duck-walked into the end zone.

"I had to make the perfect throw in front of the whole world," Favre said in *Sports Illustrated for Kids* magazine.

Holmgren said he trusted Favre to audible—sort of.

"I told him if he audibles it's fine," Holmgren said. "But they have to work, and that one worked beautifully."

Before Rison even hit pay dirt, Favre created one of the lasting images from Super Bowl XXXI. He yanked off his helmet and raced toward the New England sideline before reversing course to the Green Bay sideline, all the while holding his helmet high in triumph. This was the Super Bowl—why hold back? "It was like a home game and Mardi Gras rolled into one," Favre said.

Favre's first pass had put the Packers up 7–0 less than four minutes into the game. *Washington Times* writer Rick Snider, exaggerating only a little, said it was obvious the game was over. "You still had chips in the bag and a few cold ones in the fridge, and already you're searching for the remote control and wondering what else is on," he wrote.

The Packers boosted their lead to 10–0, but New England responded with two touchdowns to take a 14–10 advantage before the end of the first quarter. Green Bay then grabbed the momentum back, starting the second quarter even faster than it started the first. Less than a minute into the period, safety Lawyer Milloy, in man-to-man coverage, bit on a hard inside step by wide receiver Antonio Freeman. Freeman then blew past him to the outside, and Favre tossed a lob that Freeman caught along the right sideline near the 50. Freeman outran Milloy and safety Willie Clay to the end zone. A play that broke the record for the longest play from scrimmage in Super Bowl history occurred literally seconds after a TV graphic showed Green Bay averaging negative yardage on first down.

The Packers continued to pile on the points. They were leading 20–10 after a second Chris Jacke field goal when they drove the ball to the New England 2 with just over a minute left before halftime. Favre capped a nine-play, 74-yard drive by rolling left and then lunging across the goal line. The officials' call was controversial, but they ruled Favre had hit the pylon with the ball just before his knee hit the ground, putting Green Bay up 27–14 at intermission.

"We never had a doubt that we would win this ball game," Favre would say afterward.

The Patriots did climb to within six points, 27–21, on a touchdown with three-and -a-half minutes left in the third quarter. But Desmond Howard blew them out of the game 17 seconds later, returning a kickoff 99 yards for a post-season record touchdown on his way to being named Most Valuable Player of the game. Favre hit tight end Mark Chmura for a two-point conversion on the final score of the game and Green Bay held on to win, 35–21.

It was Favre's first championship on any level.

Howard had amassed 154 yards on kickoff returns and 90 yards on punt returns, both post-season records. The defense—including defensive end Reggie White, who recorded a Super Bowl-record three sacks—was stout, especially late in the game. And Favre finished with 254 yards passing, the two touchdown passes and his own rushing TD, overcoming five Patriot sacks.

Favre joking around as television broadcaster John Madden talks with Packers defensive coach Bob Valesente. The Packers were tuning up for a playoff game in San Francisco on the way to Super Bowl XXXI.

Favre shined despite having the flu with a fever on the Thursday before the game. The fever broke overnight, and the next day he vowed not to let sickness take him down. "Took my brother Scott and some friends to Bourbon Street. We ate oysters and shrimp, drank a few beers and had a big time. It was what I needed," Favre said in *Playboy*. "Got up the next day ready to play football."

The victory made things right again in the world. "The Lombardi Trophy is going home," Tony Kornheiser wrote in the *Washington Post*. "It's like Excalibur is returning to the rock…Nobody outside of Boston can be upset with this result. History and tradition are served. And hey, it's a good thing for dairy farmers."

And for Packer fans everywhere who stayed with Favre.

"I hope people didn't bet against me," Favre said of anyone who doubted his Super Bowl prediction, "because they'd be broke right now."

Blue-chip ability, charisma, the greatest competitor alive.

He's a bitch.

I just love that guy.

—Jon Gruden former
Packers assistant coach

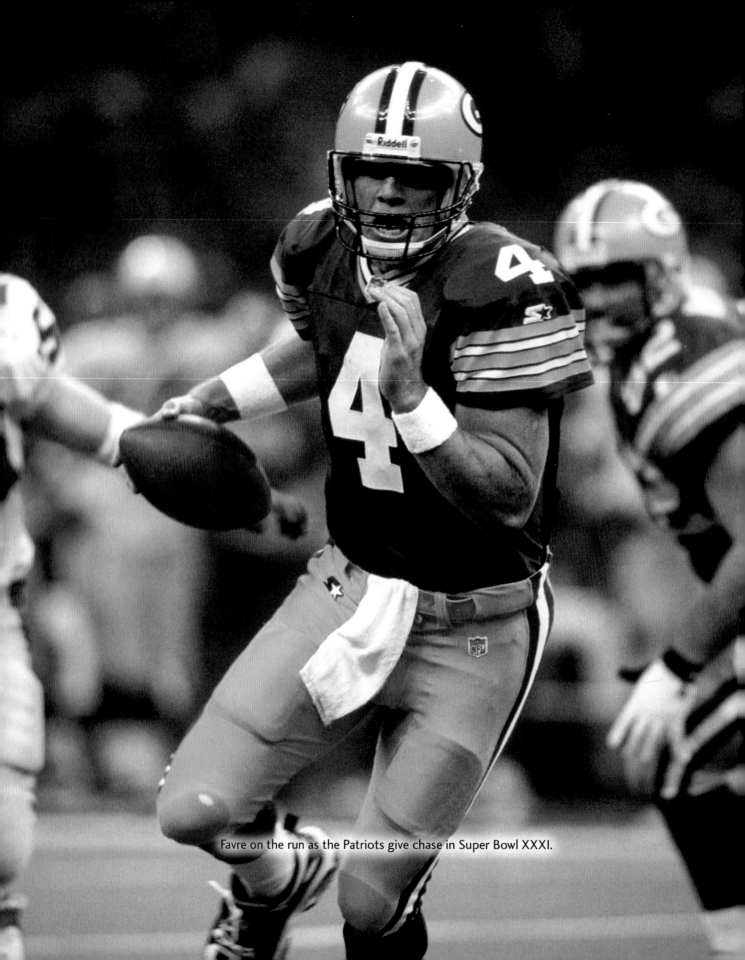

Favre on the run as the Patriots give chase in Super Bowl XXXI.

Favre being interviewed after the game by television broadcaster Terry Bradshaw as the Vince Lombardi Trophy is raised up behind them.

HEAD BUTTS AND BUTT SLAPS

Before falling to the Denver Broncos, 31–24, in Super Bowl XXXII, the Packers won playoff games against the Tampa Bay Buccaneers and the San Francisco 49ers. Both games featured memorable exchanges between Favre and D-linemen.

The divisional game at Lambeau Field was marked by feuding between Favre and one of his favorite foes, Bucs defensive lineman Warren Sapp. Sapp had a huge game, forcing two fumbles, recovering one of them, and sacking Favre three times. He harassed and taunted Favre throughout the game, and Favre responded with his own insults and head butts. Favre said he would be able to repeat only "three words" of their conversation in mixed company.

"It's kinda comical," said Packers running back Dorsey Levens, who ran for a team playoff record 112 yards and one touchdown. "The guys are swearing back and forth. And Brett doesn't back down from anyone. On one play I do remember, Sapp was getting tired, and he was going out. And Brett was like, 'That's right, go over there and take a blow.' But not in those words. Warren got pretty upset and stayed in the game."

At one point, Packers Head Coach Mike Holmgren worried that sparring would hurt Favre's concentration. "He goes, 'Hey, don't let him get to you,'" Favre recalled. "I said, 'Hey, I'm getting to them.' That's the way I look at it. I enjoy that."

It certainly wasn't all serious. The Packers cinched the 21–7 victory in the fourth quarter when Levens scored on a 2-yard run and Favre added a two-point conversion on a quarterback draw. Favre then tried a reverse dunk at the goal post. He couldn't reach the crossbar, though, and threw the ball over it instead. "I'm going to catch a lot of grief over that one," he said. "As I was halfway up, I realized, 'What am I doing? I can't jump.'"

There were light moments in the NFC Championship Game in San Francisco, too, as the Packers beat the 49ers in the playoffs for the third straight year. Near the end of the 23–10 win, Packer players donned championship hats and danced in puddles on the sideline. There had been a steady rain throughout the game, but Favre shined. He hit on 16-of-27 pass attempts for 222 yards and one touchdown—without throwing an interception. Punter Craig Hentrich may have put on the flashiest performance, dropping the ball inside the 49ers 20-yard line on each of his five punts.

Favre was in the middle of extracurricular activity in this game, too. After a sack by defensive lineman Bryant Young, Favre jumped up from the turf, slapped Young on the shoulder and pulled defensive lineman and part-time professional wrestler Kevin Greene by the face mask. Favre was grinning all the while.

"Bryant made a good hit," Favre said. "Real good. I just wanted to let him know I wasn't fazed by it. Kevin was doing a little of that wrestling crap. Jawing at me. I was just letting them know that I knew this was a fight, and I planned to be there all day. Hey, this is what makes the game fun."

The Packers being honored at the White House for their victory in Super Bowl XXXI. Reggie White is to the right of Favre; to the left are President Bill Clinton, Packers Head Coach Mike Holmgren, General Manager Ron Wolf, and Packers President Bob Harlan.

CHAPTER 6
THE STREAK

★★★★★★★★★★★

*I am going to lay my body
on that field for that team.*

—**Brett Favre** after being traded
to the Packers in February 1992

Will the NFL ever see a player who is as tough—*and* as talented—as Brett Favre?
Favre didn't play his final game until after he turned 37. But he had taken a terrible
pounding even before he turned 27.

"When he gets up every Monday," his wife, Deanna, said in 1995, "he looks like such
an old man."

And yet he played on, and on.

Even for the most ardent Packers fan, Favre's signature record—starting more than
237 regular-season games in a row—is hard to fathom.

He simply would not let his teammates down.

"Brett prides himself on showing up every Sunday and knowing deep down inside that,
'Hey, these guys depend on me, and I'm going to be there,'" said Packer safety LeRoy Butler.

"Ask people who know him," Butler added with a smile. "He's not human."

Besides being tough, Favre also had to be good enough to start so many games.
Several of his understudies—Mark Brunell, Aaron Brooks, Matt Hasselbeck—became

starters elsewhere. But none of them ever unseated Favre.

As talented as he was, what set Favre apart was guts, mettle, and moxie. He was the epitome of playing through pain.

"I never show anyone I'm hurt," he once said. "Never."

Remember these moments?

- In 1995, a blood vessel broke in Favre's esophagus after he was hit by three Pittsburgh Steeler defenders at Lambeau Field. Favre came to the sidelines coughing up blood, but Coach Mike Holmgren—after asking, How much blood?—sent him back in. On the next play, Favre threw the winning touchdown pass, clinching a division title for the Packers for the first time in twenty-three years. (Footnote: the Packers did get a little help from Steelers receiver Yancey Thigpen, who dropped a pass in the end zone with 11 seconds remaining, preserving Green Bay's 24–19 win.)

How did it feel to win the title? "Painful," Favre said with a smile, downplaying his injury. "There's something bleeding. That's all I know. I'm not a doctor. Something's probably jarred loose."

- Nearly nine years later, a week shy of his thirty-fifth birthday, Favre suffered a concussion against the New York Giants in another game at Lambeau. His head was driven into the turf on a tackle, and he left the game. But two downs later, before the coaches realized it was unsafe for Favre to continue, he put himself back in. On fourth-and-five, with a scared-to-death home crowd suddenly cheering again, Favre threw a 28-yard pass into an 18-mph wind. Wide receiver Javon Walker leaped between two defenders to catch it for a touchdown.

"It was like Superman just stepped back into the building," running back Tony Fisher said.

The touchdown was thrown right in front of our end zone seats, and we cheered as wildly as if it had clinched a playoff win. Superman? Favre doesn't have the "S" logo tattoo on his arm for nothing.

Over the years, Favre's toughness became legendary—and not only among fans and teammates.

"Most quarterbacks you hit in the head a few times, and they get kind of queasy," said San Francisco 49ers linebacker Ken Norton. "This guy, it turns him on."

Favre, looking groggy, returning to the field after conferring on the sideline on December 24, 1995. Favre needed time-outs twice during the game to recover from hits he suffered against the Pittsburgh Steelers. Favre endured and led the Packers to a 24–19 comeback win, clinching the Packers' first division title since 1972.

Favre being carted off the field after his foot was injured on a sack by Warren Sapp in a game against the Tampa Bay Buccaneers on November 19, 2000.

Favre writhing in pain after being hit by Washington Redskins linebacker Lavar Arrington on October 20, 2002, at Lambeau Field. Favre suffered a sprained lateral collateral ligament, an injury many initially feared was much worse.

Packers assistant trainer Kurt Fielding carting Favre off the field after Favre was injured in the hit by Arrington. The Packers won the *Monday Night Football* matchup 30-9. "I don't worry about getting hurt, and I don't worry about getting hit," Favre once said. "I guess I just play the game the way it's supposed to be played."

Favre said he thought his all-out style helped him, that you only get hurt when you play "tenderfoot."

"I always figured if the bone wasn't sticking out of the skin, you could play. That's what they made tape for," he said. "But maybe I'm different."

It didn't matter whether a playoff spot or only pride was at stake. Even at 36, in the last game of the 2005 season—when the Packers went 4–12—Favre upended a defender with a block on a running play.

Sitting in a Lambeau luxury box for the first time, I felt more proud of Favre on that play than I did on any others that day. How could you not be a proud fan? How many quarterbacks ever throw blocks—good ones—in any game?

Favre's father, Irvin Favre—a man whose very appearance said toughness—loved that quality in his son.

"That's what I admire most about Brett: He's a gutty kid, hard-nosed as heck," he once said. "He's a quarterback who loves to hit."

Courage was part of the training the father imparted as the son's coach. He had told Brett as a kid: "If you get hurt, you crawl off the field. When you can't crawl off the field, I'll come get you."

Two games stand out for the way Favre recovered from injuries and carried the Packers to victory. Both times, he tossed aside crutches to play.

It was another game, however—when Favre performed through wrenching emotional anguish—that must have made his father the most proud.

✶✶✶✶✶✶✶✶✶

A cast, crutches and talk of a wheelchair led at least one newspaper to declare that, "barring a medical miracle," Favre would miss the home game against the Indianapolis Colts on November 19, 2000.

Favre had gotten knocked out of the previous game, a 20–15 loss to the Tampa Bay Buccaneers on *Monday Night Football*. Defensive lineman Warren Sapp sacked him in the third quarter, driving him into the grass, grabbing his left foot and tearing off his left shoe. Favre could barely limp to the sideline.

Head Coach Mike Sherman said after the game: "He cannot walk at the present time. It's too early to tell, but I anticipate that he'll miss next week's game and maybe longer."

Favre emerged from the stadium on crutches. Backup quarterback Matt Hasselbeck said he heard Favre had also been given a wheelchair.

But on Tuesday, the day after the Buccaneers game, Favre was walking around on a removable cast. And by Thursday, he had the foot specially taped and was practicing. All he needed for the Colts game was a size-larger cleat to stuff his swollen and purple foot into.

That Lambeau Field was 27 degrees, with a 16-degree wind chill, probably motivated Favre all the more.

To erase any doubt about his mobility, Favre rolled out on the first play of the game. Then he rolled over the Colts. In the first half, Favre led three consecutive scoring marches, including two 87-yard drives for touchdowns, staking his team to a 19–0 lead.

"It's important to play if you can play," he said. "It hurt, but the guys were counting on me. It's part of the job. It's another day at the office."

Favre racked up 301 yards passing, hitting eight receivers and connecting at a 63.9 percent clip.

Crutches? Wheelchair?

Indianapolis quarterback Peyton Manning led a strong comeback, but the underdog Packers held on for a 26–24 win. Besides preserving his starting streak, Favre extended his record to 25–0 at home when the temperature was 34 degrees or below at kickoff.

"I don't know if it's the weather or the injuries that make him play better," said Hasselbeck. "But it was very Favre-esque."

Sherman, whose initial statements had caused the headlines about the streak being in jeopardy, was exuberant after the game.

"One thing you can't tell Brett Favre is that he can't do something," Sherman said. "As I told him a few minutes ago, he actually relished the fact that he had a bad foot going into the game. It was just another challenge for him. You can't tell him he can't do something. It's amazing."

Harder to measure than a victory was the lasting effect Favre's courage had on his teammates.

When your leader plays hurt—and gives an MVP-like performance—you're bound to give a little extra yourself.

"The guy is a superstar, he's a true champion," guard Ross Verba said after the Colts game. "I love playing for that guy."

Favre left another game on crutches, this time due to a severe ankle sprain, six days before the Packers faced the Chicago Bears on November 12, 1995. For two days, Favre had the injury iced and, by the third day, he also was receiving heat treatments. All week the injured area was electronically stimulated.

The most Favre could muster was taking six snaps in a passing drill on Friday and 10 snaps on Saturday. His status was so uncertain that the Packers signed as a backup Bob Gagliano, a 37-year-old quarterback who hadn't played in three years.

But come game day, with first place in the NFC Central Division on the line, Favre ran through the Lambeau Field tunnel, a cast-like accumulation of tape wrapped around his ankle.

Favre suffered a concussion after being driven to the ground by New York Giants defensive tackle William Joseph on October 3, 2004. The back of Favre's helmet slammed violently to the Lambeau Field turf. Favre went out for two plays and then, before coaches realized it was unsafe for him to return, he put himself back in the game. On fourth-and-five, into a driving wind, Favre threw a 28-yard touchdown pass to wide receiver Javon Walker before being taken out for the rest of the game.

The Streak

During the week, Bears Head Coach Dave Wannstedt had said there was no quarterback in the division he'd rather have than his own Erik Kramer. But take a wild guess on whether it was Kramer or Favre that day who:

- Completed 75 percent of his passes—25-of-33, for 336 yards and no interceptions.

- Tied a club record with five touchdown passes.

- Set what then was his career-best passer rating of 147.2.

Ailing in the bone-chilling cold with flurries falling, Favre didn't even commit a turnover.

"He was like Michael Jordan when he was hitting all of those threes and couldn't believe they were going in," said Packers Assistant Coach Steve Mariucci.

The Bears were leading 28–21 when Favre took over the game. He tied it in the third quarter with a 44-yard touchdown strike to wide receiver Robert Brooks. Then he completed 4-of-6 passes on the Packers' next possession, in the fourth quarter, moving his team through the air for 67 yards of a 69-yard drive. The drive culminated in a 16-yard touchdown pass to running back Edgar Bennett.

The 35–28 win, in the 150th meeting of the two teams, put the Packers in a tie with the Bears for first place in the NFC Central, which the Packers would later clinch.

It was a victory of the heart, wrote Dallas Morning News *columnist Rick Gosselin.*

Still, some Bears weren't impressed.

"Could you have thrown those passes?" asked Bears defensive lineman Alonzo Spellman. "Well, I could have. It had nothing to do with his great, great play."

OK, Alonzo.

"He's not Troy Aikman," snapped linebacker Vinson Smith.

Yeah, no kidding, Vinnie.

"You can talk about Favre all you want," chirped yet another discordant Bear, cornerback Jeremy Lincoln. "He's a good player, OK? Is that what you want to hear. But he's not Troy Aikman."

Hello? Do I hear an echo?

Favre hadn't known what to expect going into the game.

"I've never played in a game where I didn't practice, so I didn't know how I'd respond to the game," he said. "I told the guys, 'Hey, just protect me. If you do that, it's going to be easy on me.' It really was."

✱✱✱✱✱✱✱✱✱

Over the years, Favre kept his game-starting streak alive despite personal problems that hit in waves.

Before the 1996 season, Favre spent 46 days in treatment for his Vicodin addiction. Soon after that came news that Favre's sister, Brandi, had been involved in a drive-by shooting. And then their older brother, Scott, was convicted of felony drunken driving. He had driven into a railroad crossing, and a collision with a train killed his passenger, a close friend of Brett's.

In 2004, back-to-back tragedies struck. Deanna Favre's 24-year-old brother, Casey Tynes, died in an all-terrain vehicle accident on Favre's property near Hattiesburg, Mississippi. And less than a week later, Deanna was diagnosed with breast cancer.

Perhaps the greatest test for Favre, however, was on December 22, 2003, in a game against the Oakland Raiders on *Monday Night Football*.

It was a game, wrote Bob McGinn of the Milwaukee Journal Sentinel, *that passed immediately into legend.*

Little more than 24 hours before the Packers would meet the Raiders, Favre was golfing with backup quarterback Doug Pederson and two other teammates. Favre wasn't carrying his cell phone, so Deanna called Pederson with stunning news.

Irvin Favre had suffered a massive heart attack while driving near the family's home in Mississippi. He swerved off the road and died instantly. He was 58.

Sherman told Favre he could skip the game and go home, according to an article by Peter King in *Sports Illustrated*. But Favre stayed with the team in California.

"I said, 'Mike, I'm playing. There's no doubt in my mind that's what he would have wanted.'"

"It's almost like I could hear my dad: 'Boy, don't worry about me. I'm fine.'"

Favre spoke to the team shortly after getting the news. He began to cry as he walked to the front of the room to speak, according to *SI*.

"I loved my dad, I love football, I love you guys," Favre said. "I grew up playing baseball for my dad, and I grew up playing football for my dad. It's all I know. It's my life. I'm playing in this game because I've invested too much in the game, in you, in this team, not to play. If you ever doubted my commitment to this team, never doubt it again."

The next night, Favre had to fight through pre-game jitters like never before. For the first time, he said, he felt scared before kickoff.

"I'm thinking: 'Focus. Focus. If you're gonna play, you can't go out and lay an egg.' Everybody would have understood if I had played lousy, but my dad wouldn't have stood for any excuses."

The tension continued to mount. When Favre was introduced, Raider fans in the notorious "Black Hole" section of the stadium shocked everyone by cheering him.

"I'm hearing this, and I couldn't hardly breathe," Favre said.

Yet, Favre completed his first nine passes, and 12 of his first 13. By halftime, he had

Favre taking a quiet moment on the bench during a game against the Oakland Raiders on December 22, 2003, a day after the death of his father, Irvin Favre. Favre said he knew his father would want him to play, but the game clearly took a toll on Favre so soon after learning of his father's death.

thrown for 311 yards and four touchdowns and posted a perfect passer rating, 158.3. The Packers led 31–7, and the Raiders' spirit was crushed.

Favre did it while playing with a broken heart, as well as fractured right thumb.

What made his play even more thrilling was that—as cliché as it sounds—he seemed to get help from above.

The first touchdown pass, a 21-yard rainbow, seemed to defy physics the way it arced sharply downward to give tight-end Wesley Walls just enough room in the end zone to gather it in. And the third TD pass, a 43-yarder to receiver Javon Walker, had no business being caught. It was as if someone reached down and prevented two better-positioned defenders from touching the ball.

"At one point, I just told myself, the hell with it, I'll just throw it up there—the other team ain't touching it. And they didn't," Favre said.

The Packers won, 41–7. The Raiders had slipped badly that season, the one following their trip to the Super Bowl.

But no one had ever seen such stellar play under those circumstances.

"Favre didn't just bring honor to his own father, Irvin; he brought honor to all the kids and fathers who tossed the football or baseball in the backyard, particularly those who had to part before it was time," Michael Wilbon wrote in *The Washington Post*.

For the game, Favre was 22-of-30 (73 percent) for 399 yards and four touchdowns, with no interceptions and a passer rating of 154.9, the highest of his career. It was his most amazing performance of the 2003 season, one in which he played with the broken thumb in ten of the sixteen regular-season games. Despite the injury, he led the league with 32 touchdown passes, posted the highest completion percentage (65.4) of his career and finished second to Oakland quarterback Rich Gannon for what would have been his fourth Most Valuable Player award.

The Packers later suffered a bitter playoff loss to the Philadelphia Eagles in what fans remember as the fourth-and-twenty-six game.

But that took nothing away from a performance that remains in a class by itself.

"This was just pure, absolute willpower," center Mike Flanagan said after the Raiders game. "I've seen the Super Bowl years, I've seen the MVP years, but I've never been more impressed by a man in my life than I have been in the last 24 hours by Brett Favre. It's just amazing what he did."

On the plane ride back to Green Bay, according to *Sports Illustrated*, Favre had a big cry when he called his mother, Bonita, to see how she was doing.

She told him that, a couple of weeks before he died, Irvin had told a friend:

"You think Brett's decided who he wants to introduce him when he's inducted into the Hall of Fame? I hope he picks me."

✶✶✶✶✶✶✶✶✶✶

You can tear his arm off and he would function with the other hand.

—Ray Rhodes
former Packers coach
on Brett Favre

Guard Mark Tauscher hugging Favre during what clearly was an emotional game for all of the Packers after the death of Favre's father.

Favre celebrating in the first half in the Raiders game. In that magical half, Favre completed his first nine passes and 12 of his first 13. He threw for four touchdowns and 311 yards, and posted a perfect passer rating of 158.3.

Favre celebrating a touchdown a little more than 24 hours after the unexpected death of his father. The Packers defeated the Raiders 41–7.

Favre being embraced by wide receiver Robert Ferguson. Favre said he had an extra sense that his passes would be caught in the Raiders game. "At one point, I just told myself, the hell with it, I'll just throw it up there—the other team ain't touching it. And they didn't," he said.

Favre accepting the game ball from Head Coach Mike Sherman (background) after the Packers' win over the Raiders. Wide receiver Donald Driver (far right) looks on.

Favre breaking down after speaking to the team after the game.

ONE AND DONE

From early in the 1992 season—when Brett Favre started his first game for the Green Bay Packers—through 2005, 185 quarterbacks started games in the NFL, according to the Elias Sports Bureau. Favre was the Packers' only starter during that period. The team's division rivals, meanwhile, each had a laundry list.

CHICAGO BEARS: 20	DETROIT LIONS: 15	MINNESOTA VIKINGS: 12
Henry Burris	Charlie Batch	Todd Bouman
Chris Chandler	Stoney Case	Daunte Culpepper
Will Furrer	Ty Detmer	Randall Cunningham
Rex Grossman	Gus Frerotte	Gus Frerotte
Jim Harbaugh	Jeff Garcia	Rich Gannon
Chad Hutchinson	Joey Harrington	Jeff George
Erik Kramer	Jon Kitna	Tarvaris Jackson
Craig Krenzel	Erik Kramer	Brad Johnson
Dave Krieg	Dave Krieg	Jim McMahon
Shane Matthews	Don Majkowski	Warren Moon
Cade McNown	Mike McMahon	Sean Salisbury
Jim Miller	Scott Mitchell	Spergon Wynn
Rick Mirer	Rodney Peete	
Moses Moreno	Frank Reich	
Kyle Orton	Andre Ware	
Jonathan Quinn		
Steve Stenstrom		
Kordell Stewart		
Steve Walsh		
Peter Tom Willis		

GREEN BAY PACKERS: 1
Brett Favre

"If you say the wrong things to the media, if you're not fan friendly, if you're a bad locker room guy, if you're a guy who has an 'all about me' attitude—any one of those things will ruin you as a quarterback in this league, regardless of how good you are on the field. Being a great player is not enough for an NFL QB...

When people talk about my consecutive-game streak, they always make a big deal about how durable I've been. To me, the bigger deal is that for 10 years I've been able to handle all the things that go along with this job, and to do them so well that the Packers have never felt the need to replace me. For 10 years, the coaches and the players on this team have believed in my ability and leadership.

That, right there, is no easy feat."

— **Brett Favre**, *ESPN The Magazine*,
January 6, 2003

CHAPTER 7
RIVALS

✮✮✮✮✮✮✮✮✮

Just another game for us. Fans and media make it bigger than it is.

—Brett Favre in 1998 after beating the Chicago Bears for the ninth time in a row

If Packer fans had our own hall of fame, we would have voted Brett Favre in years ago — even if he had never won a Super Bowl or an MVP award.

Favre would get an entire wing in our hall just because of the way he punished and shamed the vile, stinking, and detestable Chicago Bears.

It hadn't always been that way, you know.

"I can remember when I first came in here," Favre said in 1996, "most of the fans were talking about 'I don't care what you do, just beat Chicago twice. You can go 2–14.'"

In the seven seasons before Favre came to the Packers, a force against God, nature, and Vince Lombardi had allowed the Bears to beat the Packers twelve out of fourteen times.

Chicago also won the first matchup of the 1992 season, in Favre's first game against the Bears. But in the teams' second meeting that season, Favre led the Packers to victory—and ever since, the Earth has once again revolved around the Sun, and God and Vince have enjoyed football again.

Favre throwing as Chicago Bears defender Chris Zorich mounts a pass rush on December 11, 1994. The Packers beat the Bears 40–3.

How the Packers mashed and mauled the Marshmallows of the Midway during the Favre era. Through 2006:

- In 30 games against the Bears, the Packers won 22 of them (73 percent).

- On the Bears' home field, Green Bay won thirteen out of fifteen (87 percent).

- From 1994 through 1998, Green Bay beat Chicago ten straight times—the longest streak in Packers-Bears history, which dates back to 1921 and is the oldest rivalry in the NFL.

Give Favre the credit.

"He's the chairman of the board, the best of the best, the Mac-Daddy of football," said Bears Defensive Coordinator Greg Blache, who had been a Packers assistant. "If you're going to start a franchise, that's the guy I would start with. The guy's worth eight, nine wins [a season] himself. He's probably the scariest guy in football."

The suffering that Bears fans endured almost makes you sad for them. At one point, former Bear Doug Buffone, a talk show host on Chicago sports radio, seemed ready to forfeit rather than play the Packers.

"Favre is just murdering us. He's a killer," Buffone said. "We've tried every trick in the book to get him, but every time he plays us, it's like he owns us. We've never shut him down.

"I swear he goes into every season saying: 'OK, I have two wins in the bag, so all I have to do is pull off fourteen more.'"

How sad, no? The Packers had become to the Bears, wrote *Chicago Sun-Times* columnist Rick Telander, what "a six-lane highway is to a roving groundhog."

It got so bad, in fact, that in 2003, when Favre whipped the Bears in the first game at newly renovated Soldier Field, one Chicago writer openly wished that the stadium had been rebuilt with only obstructed-view seats.

It's easy to understand why. Through 2006:

- Favre threw at least one touchdown pass *against the Bears* in 25 consecutive games—an NFL record.

- Favre threw more touchdowns—52—*against the Bears* than against any other team.

- And Favre used the Bears to create his own single-game record book most completions, 36—*against the Bears;* most passing yards, 402—*against the Bears;* longest touchdown pass, 99 yards—*against the Bears;* and most touchdown passes, five—*against the Bears* (and two other teams).

As one-sided as Favre had made things, it was surprising that Wisconsin sports fans still ranked the Packers and Bears as the state's biggest sports rivalry in a 2003 *Sports*

Illustrated poll.

Maybe a rivalry is best when you keep beating the you-know-what out of the team you hate the most.

BRETT FAVRE'S 10* BEST VICTORIES OVER THE BEARS:
Through 2006. Another was Favre's incredible performance against the Bears after being on crutches a few days before the game. (See Chapter 6—The Streak.)

NOVEMBER 22, 1992
PACKERS 17, BEARS 3 AT SOLDIER FIELD

Before this game, *Chicago Tribune* columnist Bernie Lincicome put Favre in a league with Don Majkowski, the man Favre replaced, and the Packers' other quarterback, Mike Tomczak. It was doubtful, Lincicome wrote, that Favre would be "any more of a long-range savior than Don Majkowski was before him."

Typical dumb Bears fan.

In the second Packers-Bears contest of '92, with Green Bay ahead 10–3 early in the fourth quarter, Favre led a 13-play, 74-yard scoring march that put the game away. He went 5-for-5 for 53 yards on the 9-minute drive, which he punctuated with a 5-yard dash for his first career touchdown. Favre chose to run—chased by Bears linemen Richard Dent, Steve McMichael, and William "The Refrigerator" Perry—despite having dislocated his left shoulder the previous week, when Philadelphia Eagles defensive end Reggie White slammed him to the ground.

"I didn't even think about it," Favre said of his shoulder injury. "At that stage of the game, anything goes."

Chicago, which had beaten Green Bay five straight times, took the loss hard. In the locker room, the Bears huddled together, a Chicago reporter wrote, "like victims of a devastating natural disaster."

They would get used to the feeling.

OCTOBER 31, 1993
PACKERS 17, BEARS 3 AT LAMBEAU FIELD

The Packers were tenacious, sacking Bears quarterback Jim Harbaugh seven times and leaving him with bruises on his back, scratches on his legs and swelling on an ankle—a week after he'd been sacked nine times by the Minnesota Vikings.

Even Favre hit hard that day. Packers running back Darrell Thompson had barely

FAVRE'S FAVORITE FOE

Brett Favre reached some of his biggest
milestones in games against the Chicago Bears:

November 7, 1999

Broke Ron Jaworski's record of 116 consecutive
starts by an NFL quarterback.

December 9, 2001

Became the first quarterback in NFL history to pass
for 3,000 yards in 10 consecutive seasons.

October 7, 2002

Reached 40,000 career yards in passing in a win at
Champaign, Illinois, on *Monday Night Football.*

been touched on a touchdown sweep—until Favre leveled him from behind in the end zone in one of his characteristically rough TD celebrations.

"I was so excited, and after I hit him I thought, 'What the hell did I just do?'" Favre said.

OCTOBER 31, 1994
PACKERS 33, BEARS 6 AT SOLDIER FIELD

The teams wore throwback jerseys from the 1920s on a Halloween night haunted by a wind chill of 8 degrees, wind gusts more than 50 miles per hour and rain coming down in sheets. More than half of the Soldier Field fans left by halftime—when the Bears retired the numbers of team legends Dick Butkus and Gale Sayers.

(Nice loyalty, you Flatlanders.)

Favre was the star in the storm, scampering for 22 yards on one carry and scoring from 36 yards on another.

"The last time I ran one in like that was the fifth grade," he said of his touchdown.

SEPTEMBER 11, 1995
PACKERS 27, BEARS 24 AT SOLDIER FIELD

Green Bay let the Bears stay close this time but still burned them on *Monday Night Football.*

Favre tied an NFL record with a 99-yard touchdown pass to Robert Brooks on a third-and-ten play. "The play was beautifully constructed," wrote Tom Silverstein of the *Milwaukee Journal Sentinel.* "Brooks ran a slant and Favre pump faked, drawing in cornerback Donnell Woolford. Brooks broke it back outside and hauled in Favre's pass at about the Packers' 40. No one came close to catching him."

That's when Favre got dangerous again. Racing down the sideline to celebrate the TD, he knocked Packers safety LeRoy Butler flat. "Nearly gave me a concussion," Butler said.

OCTOBER 6, 1996
PACKERS 37, BEARS 6 AT SOLDIER FIELD

Favre threw four touchdown passes, including a 50-yard Hail Mary off his back foot to wide receiver Antonio Freeman to end the first half. "They're going to watch that film and say, 'Holy…,'" Butler said, finishing his thought with a smile. It was Green Bay's fifth straight victory over Chicago and, at the time, the longest such streak against the Bears since a five-game string from 1960 to '62 during the Lombardi era.

"It's reached the point where every game, every quarter, every drive, every play, you expect him to do something wondrous," Head Coach Mike Holmgren said of Favre. "That's not really fair. You've got to remember, he's still a kid."

An article by Gene Collier of the *Pittsburgh Post-Gazette* put the Packers' new dominance in perspective. Going into the game, the Packers and Bears had played 150 times, and the average differential in the final score was 1.83 points. But in Favre's five-game winning streak over the Bears, Green Bay had won by an average of 22 points.

Favre had helped sink the Bears to a new low. One Milwaukee reporter estimated that nearly half of the Soldier Field crowd was wearing cheeseheads or other Packers garb. Bears linebacker Bryan Cox moaned after the massacre, "We've got to get some damned heart. It's a line in *The Wizard of Oz*. Some of our guys have to go see the Wizard because we don't have a lot of heart."

Favre had ripped it out. But some Bears remained unconvinced.

"I've seen better quarterbacks," defensive lineman Alonzo Spellman said of Favre. *Yeah, right.*

SEPTEMBER 1, 1997
PACKERS 38, BEARS 24 AT LAMBEAU FIELD

Boxing announcer Michael Buffer kicked off the *Monday Night Football* season opener with his rousing, "Let's get ready to rrrrrumble!" In the fourth quarter, the moaner Cox put that call into action. In the space of 23 seconds, he was called for three penalties, including unsportsmanlike conduct for throwing his helmet 20 yards downfield. After the game, he got into a screaming match with fans and police when a fan spit on him as he entered the locker room tunnel.

"Cox displayed about as little class as people in Green Bay believe all Chicagoans have," wrote columnist Mike Imrem of the suburban Chicago *Daily Herald*. Imrem sounded about as frustrated, if not as angry, as Cox.

"Yeah, someday Wisconsin will have its weight problem under control, Gabrielle Reece [the volleyball star and model] will call me up for a date and Bryan Cox will begin behaving himself. Then, yes, maybe it'll be time for the Bears to beat the Packers," he wrote.

As late as the 2-minute warning in the first half, the game was tied at 11, and the Packers had gained just 45 yards. But then Favre hit Brooks on a 44-yard post pattern and found him again in the end zone before halftime. That gave the Packers an 18–11 lead and the momentum to pull away in the second half.

BRETT FAVRE AGAINST THE BEARS

The Green Bay Packers dominated the Chicago Bears during the Brett Favre era, winning 73% of the matchups featuring the NFL's oldest rivals.

1992
Oct. 25   Lost 30–10 in Green Bay
Nov. 22   **Won 17–3 in Chicago**

1993
Oct. 31   **Won 17–3 in Green Bay**
Dec. 5   Lost 30–17 in Chicago

1994
Oct. 31   **Won 33–6 in Chicago**
Dec. 11   **Won 40–3 in Green Bay**

1995
Sept. 11   **Won 27–24 in Chicago**
Nov. 12   **Won 35–28 in Green Bay**

1996
Oct. 6   **Won 37–6 in Chicago**
Dec. 1   **Won 28–17 in Green Bay**

1997
Sept. 1   **Won 38–24 in Green Bay**
Oct. 12   **Won 24–23 in Chicago**

1998
Dec. 13   **Won 26–20 in Green Bay**
Dec. 27   **Won 16–13 in Chicago**

Source: Packers.com

1999
Nov. 7   Lost 14–3 in Green Bay
Dec. 5   **Won 35–19 in Chicago**

2000
Oct. 1   Lost 27–24 in Green Bay
Dec. 3   **Won 28–6 in Chicago**

2001
Nov. 11   **Won 20–12 in Chicago**
Dec. 9   **Won 17–7 in Green Bay**

2002
Oct. 7   **Won 34–21 in Champaign, Il.**
Dec. 1   **Won 30–20 in Green Bay**

2003
Sept. 29   **Won 38–23 in Chicago**
Dec. 7   **Won 34–21 in Green Bay**

2004
Sept. 19   Lost 21–10 in Green Bay
Jan. 2 (2005)   **Won 31–14 in Chicago**

2005
Dec. 4   Lost 19–7 in Chicago
Dec. 25   Lost 24–17 in Green Bay

2006
Sept. 10   Lost 26–0 in Green Bay
Dec. 31   **Won 26–7 in Chicago**

DECEMBER 5, 1999
PACKERS 35, BEARS 19 AT SOLDIER FIELD

The Bears made it into the second half trailing only 21–19, but then Favre broke their backs with an 11-play, 88-yard touchdown drive. Overall, Favre wasn't stellar—but he was clutch. It was a cold and rainy day in Chicago, with winds gusting to 30 miles per hour. Yet on third downs, Favre completed 7-of-10 passes for 109 yards and a touchdown.

NOVEMBER 11, 2001
PACKERS 20, BEARS 12 AT SOLDIER FIELD

Even when the Bears were good, Favre cut them down. Going into this game, the Bears had won six straight, including overtime victories in the previous two weeks on Mike Brown interceptions that were returned for touchdowns.

After an early interception in this game, Bears fans taunted Favre. He responded with two highlight-film touchdown passes: a 41-yard bomb to wide receiver Bill Schroeder in the back left corner of the end zone just before halftime; and a 9-yard laser beam to Freeman midway through the third quarter.

"It's nice to know I've still got a little bit left in the arm," the 32-year-old Favre said with a grin.

The Bears went 13–3 that season—but they were losers in both games against the Packers.

OCTOBER 7, 2002
PACKERS 34, BEARS 21 AT CHAMPAIGN, ILLINOIS

The crying from Chicago sportswriters came even before the game this time.

"Favre has almost single-handedly turned Chicago into a bitter football town since arriving in Green Bay," wrote *Sun-Times* columnist Jay Mariotti. "Worse, he has rescued the dignity of those hopeless morons who wear foam cheese on their heads."

Soldier Field was closed in 2002—for renovation, the Bears said, but you had to wonder if it wasn't because of Favre's domination over them. The Bears played their home games at the University of Illinois that season.

Favre made the Bears' temporary digs feel just like Soldier Field by blitzing them for 359 passing yards and three first-half touchdowns. His first quarter was one of his best quarters ever: He completed 8-of-11 passes for 180 yards with two touchdowns and a quarterback rating of 154.4 (perfect is 158.3).

Favre cheering on his team during a 30–20 win over the Chicago Bears on December 1, 2002. Favre said that when he first arrived in Green Bay, people told him they didn't care about how many games he won—as long as he beat the Bears.

SEPTEMBER 29, 2003
PACKERS 38, BEARS 23 AT SOLDIER FIELD

The Packers ruined the Bears' debut in the new Soldier Field—"a spaceship on stilts," some said—by beating them soundly on *Monday Night Football*. Chicago got within eight points in the fourth quarter, but Favre put the game away with a 9-yard touchdown pass to wide receiver Javon Walker with 8:51 remaining and a 1-yarder to tight-end Bubba Franks with 4:21 left.

New York Times writer Thomas George captured the hideousness of the new stadium and the helplessness of the Chicago Bears.

"The renovated Soldier Field has been called everything from a flying saucer to a toilet bowl, and a mismatch in style between *Star Trek* and an old Western movie," he wrote. "Descriptions of these current Bears have been even more crude."

After the game, things got ugly again in Chicago:

"A huge game [and] we just embarrassed ourselves one more time," said Bears linebacker Brian Urlacher. "We went out there and laid a big one."

Butkus, the Bears' Hall of Fame linebacker, had visited with Favre on the field before the game. "It was about as close as any Bear got to him the rest of the night," wrote Don Pierson of the *Chicago Tribune*.

Pierson also offered a suggestion for any discussion of naming rights for Soldier Field: "Brett Favre's Playpen."

Going into the game, Butkus had had a premonition, flashing back to the stormy 1994 game at Soldier Field, when most of the crowd fled before he and Sayers could be honored at halftime.

"I remembered the night I got my number retired and that storm hit and I started thinking, 'Something bad is going to happen,'" he said.

The same feeling, no doubt, that Bears fans experienced every time they faced Brett Favre.

✮✮✮✮✮✮✮✮✮✮

He makes throws falling backward off the wrong foot underneath your armpit.

—**Greg Blache**, Chicago Bears defensive coordinator, on Brett Favre

Favre rolling out in a 34–21 win over the Bears on December 7, 2003 at Green Bay.

NEW NEMESIS: THE VIKINGS

The Chicago Bears were so bad during most of Brett Favre's days in Green Bay that the Minnesota Vikings made a strong challenge to replace them as the Packers' top rival. The Vikings played the Packers about even, but Favre still had his moments.

October 22, 1995: Packers win 38–21. Favre completed 22-of-43 passes for 295 yards, with four touchdowns and no interceptions. "Did you see how Brett responded to every bit of pressure today? He's our Terry Bradshaw," said wide receiver Charles Jordan. "This is his team. He's the prankster. He's the leader. He's the man."

December 22, 1996: Packers win 38–10. It was the Vikings' worst loss in a decade. The game had been tied at 10 when the Packers got the ball to start the third quarter. Favre put the game away by leading Green Bay to three touchdowns on three consecutive possessions.

September 21, 1997: Packers win 38–32. Favre had four touchdown passes in the first three games of the season. Then came the Vikings and, for the third time in his career, Favre threw five touchdown passes—four of them in a 17-minute span in the first half. It must have felt extra good, because the Vikings defense had taunted him and repeatedly hit him after plays were blown dead.

Diane Pucin of the *Philadelphia Inquirer* described the scene:

First, Jeff Brady took an extracurricular pounding on Brett Favre's head. Then John Randle chose to send his helmet, with his head still in it, straight into Favre's neck and chin—after the whistle had blown the play dead. These two nasty hits were ugly and mean-spirited, but in some way understandable. It is just so frustrating to watch Favre be so perfect, watch the Green Bay quarterback zinging the football, throwing five touchdown passes, making big plays seem easy, taking away your heart and then your brains and leaving you with only one emotion—anger.

September 26, 1999 and November 6, 2000: Packers win dramatic come-from-behind victories. (See Chapter 2—Comebacks.)

December 17, 2000: Packers win 33–28. Favre came into the game with a 1–7 record at the Metrodome, with just five touchdowns and 12 interceptions. He didn't throw any picks in this game, connecting on 26-of-38 passes for 290 yards and three touchdowns. The Packers scored on 7-of-9 drives, including four of their first five.

"I was jacked, but I think I played as smart as I possibly could have today," Favre said.

November 12, 2006, and December 21, 2006: Packers win 23–17 and 9–7. The victories put Favre over .500 (15-14) all-time against the Vikings. The first '06 game might have been Favre's best-ever against Minnesota—and it came in the dome, normally a hostile place for Favre. In an error-free performance, Favre posted a passer rating of 100, hitting seven receivers for 347 yards and two touchdowns. Receiver Donald Driver had a career-high 191 receiving yards, including an 82-yard TD catch. After that score, Favre raced to the end zone, picked up Driver and put him onto his shoulder. "I love that guy," Driver said. "I know what he's thinking. He knows what I'm thinking. That's a great combination. When it's all said and done, I'm just glad I'll be a part of his legacy."

Favre doing a "fireman's carry" of receiver Donald Driver in San Francisco after a touchdown against the 49ers on December 10, 2006.

Favre prepares to launch a pass in a 31–24 win over the Minnesota Vikings on December 24, 2004. Compared with Soldier Field, which one Chicago writer said should be named "Brett Favre's Playpen" because of his dominance on the Bears' home field, Favre struggled at the Metrodome.

AFTERWORD

★★★★★★★★★★

I'm a lucky guy...

For more than 14 seasons, I've watched from the sidelines as Brett Favre has done incredible things on the field: Last-minute victories, overtime wins, shovel passes that your high school coach would tell you not to try, throwing off your back foot or with no feet on the ground at all, with both eyes closed. In the rain, in the snow, in the cold, Brett Favre makes great images for a photographer. But more than once, I've put down my camera and just watched him in amazement.

He's taken a beating; broken thumb, twisted ankles and knees, a concussion. I've seen him carted off the field and walking with crutches. Even with the injuries, when it's time to play football, you just know Brett Favre will be the first person out of the locker room door. He motivates by his actions.

I've been lucky to see Brett Favre off the field, too.

I've seen Brett hold court in the locker room before the game, telling stories that you hope are true. Deer hunting season in Wisconsin? Brett has a story about the one he just missed. It seems like the same story as last year, only better. On the field, it's not uncommon to find the referees gathered around Brett before kickoff. They shake his hand and share a laugh. Referees like Brett Favre.

When it comes to jokes, meet "Brett the Cable Guy." I sit just a row or two away from Brett on the plane to road games. More than once, I've found the name tag that designates my seat attached to the middle of my back—with other players' name tags, too. When I look at Brett, I get that "Who, me?" look.

I've fallen more than once for his look-up-in-the-sky-and-watch-out-for-the-falling-football joke. You'd swear a football is about to land on your head. He pulls it off with the precision of a surgeon. When Brett is around, I've learned to watch my back, but with a smile on my face.

Brett Favre: A Packer Fan's Tribute

I've been lucky to see the soft side of Brett Favre.

When we played in Minnesota in 2003, a young boy in a wheelchair had a visit with Brett after the game. While the trainer taped his swollen thumb, Brett carried on a conversation with this boy for 20 minutes. Not because he had to, but because he wanted to. It made a great photo, it made the boy's day, and it made my day, too.

Brett the player, Brett the personality, Brett the man…we'll never see another Brett Favre. If you've watched Brett Favre play football, you should consider yourself lucky, too.

—Jim Biever
Green Bay Packers team photographer

Favre visiting with a disabled boy after a game in Minnesota against the Vikings in November 2003.

Favre waves to fans at Lambeau Field before entering the tunnel after the final game of the 2005 season. In 1999, Ron Wolf, the Packers general manager and the man who brought Favre to Green Bay, said: "I'll say it with no apologies to anyone. Brett Favre is the greatest player to have ever played in Lambeau Field."

"There will come a time when Brett Favre can no longer play. This is not that time. But at the end of this season—or the next or the next or the next—he will step away at last, having earned the peace of an endless off-season. The cold and the snow will overtake Green Bay, and the stadium at this edge of the world will stand empty behind us, the last thing we see in the rearview mirror as we cross that river, the light at last failing in the trees.

"But until that moment, Brett Favre will be throwing, in a way, for us all. Throwing hope forward, in a single clean step or with a motion as rushed and awkward as man falling out of the tub, as hurried and off-balance as the rest of us. Banking on the past while trying to read a second or two into his future, drilling clean arcs on our behalf into the weakening light and the rising odds, every stand he makes in the pocket another little long shot fired against the infinite and inevitable. Every throw a moment for hope, a defiant line, bright in the air, against chaos and diminishment and the final goodbye."

—Jeff MacGregor, *Sports Illustrated*
December 4, 2006

FAN TRIBUTES

★★★★★★★★★★

For the second edition of this book, we asked fans to write tributes
to Brett Favre. Fans from all over the country responded.

I grew up in the '60s with the old Pack. Our heroes were Starr, Taylor, Hornung, Nitschke, and, of course, Vince. But nothing compares to how we feel about Brett and his dedication to the game and how he plays it. We laughed and cried along with him during his career, and he will never know the admiration and affection all fans have around the world for his example. There will never be another like him to walk this earth and he will live in our hearts forever.

—**Alan Collins, 62**
Waukesha, Wisconsin

On Super Bowl morning 2006, Brett Favre paid a surprise visit to 30 mobilized soldiers at Camp Shelby, Mississippi, who had gathered for a touch football game. Brett showed up in a Saturn and still in his hunting clothes and chatted for 30 minutes with soldiers deploying to, or training others for, Iraq. He threw a few passes that had his trademark zip. Surprisingly, all were completed. Mr. Favre removed his hat without prompting as we saluted him, a fellow warrior, with a plaque from our brigade with the words, "Got 'er done for 241." (True fans count playoff games, too.) Brett Favre supports the troops, and none of us will forget it!

—**Lt. Col. Charles Olsen, 42**
West Bend, Wisconsin

Lt. Col. Charles Olsen presents Brett Favre with the "Got 'er Done for 241" plaque in 2006.

Fan Tributes

I never watched football until Brett Favre started playing for the Green Bay Packers. I have children his age, and I always considered him one of them.

—Carol Marvin, retiree
Whitewater, Wisconsin

Brett Favre blankets the walls of my classroom. I am a middle school teacher and coach. In my teaching and coaching, Brett stands for toughness, resiliency, and a never-say-die, never-give-up attitude. I tell my kids (many of whom are Vikings fans) I want them to be surrounded by winners. Personally, when I look around my room, I, too, am reminded to keep working hard, have fun and be the best.

—Trent Snyder, 30
Minneapolis, Minnesota

The thought of his retirement forces us to admit
A profound fear we try hard to shield:
Will we ever care this much again
When he's no longer on the field?

—Julie Lain, 31
Dallas, Texas

Julie Lain

Brett, you don't know it, but you are a part of my family. We all feel like we know you and love you as a personal friend.

—**Barbara Clauder, 61**
Madison, Wisconsin

I've coached 35 years of football, 37 years of basketball, nine years of intramurals and 43 years of baseball. Since Brett Favre came along, he's been my role model for an athlete who gives his all despite the odds, the pain, the standings, etc. No matter what, he's left it all on the field. No matter what sport, my players have always agreed.

—**Bob Wirth, 70**
Glendale, Wisconsin

As I grow up and slowly begin to realize that Brett will not play until he is 100, the one thing about No. 4 that I will never forget is that he gave me a hero to look up to, a leader to model myself after, and a player whose passion and heart for the game will never be forgotten.

—**Rob Petrie, 17**
Brookfield, Wisconsin

In 1996 I was in a nasty mountain bike accident that left me paralyzed from the waist down. Oddly enough I was on my way to watch a Packer game at a sports bar when I was hit by a truck. Sometime during my horrible stay in the hospital a reporter came in and interviewed me. The article was published the Tuesday after that glorious Packer victory the last week of January 1997. I think Brett Favre was the most-wanted commodity in America that week. But he read the article, found out where I was and sent me a letter with a signed lithograph. This is one sports hero who honest-to-God gives a damn about his fans.

—**Tom Haig, 45**
Portland, Oregon

For my birthday, my partner got us tickets to see the Packers come to Oakland to play the Raiders on *Monday Night Football* on December 22, 2003. The game started, and Brett lit it up! I looked around and saw the stunned and silent Raiders fans. Every time Brett threw the ball, his receivers went above and beyond themselves to make sure they caught it—it was like they were paying tribute to Brett and helping him say goodbye to his dad. Gradually, the Raiders fans began to realize that what they were seeing was something special, and pretty soon they were all jumping out of their seats and cheering with me as Favre completed one pass after another. The guy next to me high-fived me after a Packers touchdown pass and said, "We're seeing history tonight." What a way to pay tribute to your father.

—**Tom D'Acquisto, 41**
Hayward, California

Fan Tributes

We tucked our jersey under our church clothes every Sunday.

—Nicholas L. Honeck, 24
Oak Creek, Wisconsin

I was in line to get Brett's autograph, and Brett just chatted away with me like we were old friends. I was so impressed that a multimillionaire would sit there and talk with an old lady like me. I love him as our QB, but I really appreciated his humble attitude toward the fans.

—Betty "Grannypacker" Sweeney, 67
Plover, Wisconsin

I was driving through Mississippi soon after Favre was traded to the Packers. I put on my Packers hat and T-shirt and proceeded to Kiln. There were two convenience stores, so I picked one and asked if this was the hometown of the Packers' next star quarterback. The clerk asked me where I was from, and I told her I was from Green Bay (which I am) and she said she had to make a phone call. We chatted for a few minutes and then a fellow came in and said "Is this the fellow asking about Brett?" It was Irvin Favre! He was driving a drivers education car and could not have been nicer. He said I was the first "tourist" to come to Kiln because of Brett. We talked about how great the Packers were going to be now, and he assured me I would have an autographed picture in my mailbox when I got home to Georgia. Sure enough, not only was there a picture but a full-page handwritten letter from Brett saying he didn't have a picture yet with the Packers but he sent one of himself with the Falcons. He said he hoped he would be able to pay back the Packers for their faith in him to trade away a No. 1 pick. I still have that letter in a frame!!

—Barry Raab, 44
St. Simons Island, Georgia

Barry Raab with his collection of Packers memorabilia.

I was born and raised in Wisconsin, and hence, a Packer fan all of my life. My career has resulted in my living outside of Wisconsin for the last 21 years. However, my five kids have been raised as avid Packer fans, as well. They love Favre. What a great role model he is for them, as they are all athletes. He has showed them how to love the game, how to give 100 percent in every game/practice, how to be loyal to your team, and how to take responsibility for mistakes.

—**Kevin Alberts, 44**
Naperville, Illinois

In April 1996, I was a part-time photographer, and I was sent to take pictures of an autograph session Brett Favre did at a shopping mall. A new family walked up to Brett. The mom and dad were obviously eagerly waiting for this moment. The dad handed over what could only have been a few-days-old newborn dressed in a teeny football-shaped jumper. The baby was sleeping, and its head was sticking out of a hole in the front of the "football" with white laces stitched down the length of his tummy. Brett held the tiny baby in his large arm and smiled so sweetly.

—**Renee Salus, 30**
Madison, Wisconsin

I want to thank Brett Favre for all of the time I spent with my son Jesse watching Favre play and making it easier for me to teach Jesse that, when a situation arises that seems to be impossible, Brett always tried to make something positive out of it. Almost every game, I could point out a play, from an averted sack that turned into positive yardage to fighting through the pain of an injury and leading the team on a successful drive, Brett always tried to make the most out of the situation. I always used his efforts as a parenting tool to help me teach my son during our Packer Game Quality Time. Thanks, Brett!

—**Dave Gall, 44**
Cedarburg, Wisconsin

As a young girl in Minnesota, I proudly sported my No. 4 jersey to school after each game and had a Favre poster hanging in my green and gold bedroom. I love every single time he would sprint the length of the field just to pick up his receiver, who had just caught one of his rocket-like passes and took it all the way for a touchdown—and his amazing smile after an all-star performance.

—**Elizabeth Kassulke, 23**
Honolulu, Hawaii

Brett Favre has been the strongest force in the last 15 years of my life besides Jesus Christ and my parents.

—**Michael Kempinski, 23**
Whitewater, Wisconsin

Cheering for Brett is something that I share with my 7-year-old daughter, Mina. His never-quit mentality and passion is something I hope to instill in her. As he walked off the field after his last game in 2006, my daughter, in tears, asked "If he retires, who are we going to root for?" I told her, "It will be all right," we will always root for the Packers, and we will always root for Brett Favre."

—**Boyd Barsness, 36**
Albertville, Minnesota

Boyd Barsness and
his daughter, Mina.

The day the Packers traded for Brett, I went to three sports cards shops and bought all of the Brett Favre cards they had—18 rookie cards for $8.50. That's a deal. The rest is history.

—**Tom Oldani, 63**
Kenosha, Wisconsin

Tom Oldani poses with his sports card collection.

When I was a young boy living in California, I would watch my beloved Packers whenever possible on a snowy, obscure UHF channel on my black-and-white TV. I cried when they carted Bart Starr off the field and straight to the hospital toward the end of his career. Twenty-plus years later, Brett Favre made me cry again, this time with tears of joy, watching the Packers hoist the Lombardi Trophy as champions of Super Bowl XXXI.

—Charlie Saporito, 46
Morgan Hill, California

Aug. 8, 1992, was the first day I loved football. I was 7 years old and knew nothing about the game, but I was at Lambeau Field with my dad for Brett Favre's first preseason game with the Packers. My memories of that game are faint, but since that day I have gone from an admiring child to an adult. To this day, when I watch him play, I am taken back to that warm August afternoon, and I feel like a kid again.

—Cherie Scharfenberg, 22
Fountain, Colorado

I thought it was commendable, but not that big of a deal, when Brett shaved his head after Deanna was diagnosed with breast cancer. The following spring, my mom was diagnosed with breast cancer. Then I realized what Brett did showed that he was as big a man off the field as he was on. Thanks to Brett, I, too, was inspired and shaved my head for my mom the day I met her for her first chemo treatment.

—Jack Copet, 31
West Allis, Wisconsin

Jack Copet

The best thing I remember about Favre is that he saved me from gutting my entire house. Every time they lost, I ripped out a wall on the second floor. With Favre, they finally started winning and I finished the upstairs remodeling.

—Neil Sass, 44
Cedarburg, Wisconsin

With only 1 minute and 7 seconds left and the Packers trailing 23–17, Favre hits Kitrick Taylor down the right side line for his first career come-from-behind win. I'll never forget playing football against my little brother in the yard and yelling out those exact words, "Kitrick Taylor down the ride sideline," every time I broke away for a touchdown!

—Bradley Gumz, 27
Minneapolis, Minnesota

Bradley Gumz

While some debate who should be considered the greatest quarterback ever, there is no debate about which provided the greatest theater. Brett Favre captivated because, in his prime, we didn't know what was coming next. A shovel pass at the goal line? A bullet over the middle? The famous "jump fake" pass handoff? They joy was never knowing what he would treat us to this Sunday. And knowing he'd be there to offer an encore the one after that.

—Richard Mueller, 42
Evansville, Indiana

In September 1992, when I was in eighth grade, Brett Favre came in for the injured Don Majkowski and the rest is history. Fast forward 15 years and I have a college degree, have my own business, and married with a baby born in early 2007, and Brett Favre is still playing football for the Green Bay Packers. Although I don't know Brett personally, I feel as though he is a big part of my life.

—Tim Evans, 28
Palatine, Illinois

Tim Evans

After attending my first Packer game in December 1969—and watching Don Horn break Bart Starr's records with five touchdowns and 410 yards passing—I remember telling my dad that he was "way better" than Bart Starr. My father just said, "There will never be a better quarterback in Green Bay than Bart Starr." I hate to echo the same sentiment to my son, Jimmy, as we have headed to section 124 for each game. But something tells me we will never see a better quarterback in Green Bay than Brett Favre. I just won't tell my son that. Leave him with hope.

—Will Tippet, 45
Winnetka, Illinois

Abby Butterfield with Brett Favre in 1995.

My family and I were at a Milwaukee Wave soccer game in one of the suites, around 1995, and Brett was there for a promotion. My daughter, Abby, who was about seven at the time, wandered out and wandered right into the suite where Brett was watching the game. Instead of asking her to leave, Brett invited her to have her picture taken with him, and we eventually had it autographed and framed, and it is one of her most prized possessions. I just thought that was one of the nicest gestures in a time when most pro athletes are way too full of themselves to do anything that they are not being paid to do.

—Mike Butterfield, 51
Wauwatosa, Wisconsin

Fan Tributes

The thing that will define Brett Favre is the passion, the exuberance, and the sheer love of the game of football. I'll remember all the broken plays that turned into gold, all the wild blocks on reverses that made us all cringe, the 40-yard rockets on a line between three defenders, the great performances playing through injuries, running around on the field like a little kid, the goofy grins after ridiculous plays and playing his greatest game of his life under the most difficult circumstances. Those are the things that will define Brett Favre. That is the stuff of legend.

—Dan Kowalsky, 17
Menomonee Falls, Wisconsin

In Wisconsin, if Brett Favre were to run for God, the incumbent would start out 40 points behind in the polls.

—Richard S. Russell, 62
Madison, Wisconsin

My husband and I have had Packer tickets for over 40 years. During the Lombardi era, my husband would always say, "You will never see football played like this again." RIGHT, until Brett Favre put the word FUN back into playing football. He is like a kid in a candy store— eager, happy, and excited—every moment he is on the field. He is the Green Bay Packers. There will never be another one like him.

—Marta Roach, 70
Elm Grove, Wisconsin

My favorite plays are when he gets to block on an end-around. He seems to really get excited about making a good block.

—Don Hartman, 65
Osceola, Wisconsin

Don Hartman

Hailey Kertscher

When Brett Favre plays, he plays to win. To lose, he is sad, but he also lets it go and puts the rest of his energy into the next game. I like that!

—Hailey Kertscher, 8
Milwaukee, Wisconsin

FAVRE QUOTES

HIS STYLE OF PLAY

"As much as everyone hates to take chances, I *love* to, even when it gets me in trouble."

—*Los Angeles Times,*
January 9, 1994

"I hate watching [game] films because sometimes I wonder, 'What the hell am I doing?'"

—*Los Angeles Times,*
January 9, 1994

Commenting on how Steve Young watched film of him to get tips on how to run the 49ers' offense:
"God help him."

—*USA Today,*
January 23, 1998

"Sometimes, I can make plays when plays are not there. Or I can get a pass off when a guy is coming at my back. Like eyes in the back of your head. I feel I have that. Guys say, 'How did you see that?' Well, I didn't. I just kind of felt it. It's instincts."

—*Tampa Tribune,*
October 11, 1999

"I never cheat myself and my teammates in any way. (Packers Head Coach Mike) Holmgren used to always say, 'Concede a play every once in a while. You don't have to (try to) score on every play, you don't have to block, you don't have to tackle.' I feel differently. You never know what play is going to be the most important play of the game."

—*Wisconsin State Journal,*
September 19, 1999

"I would not tell any young quarterback to emulate the way I throw, the way I play. To say I'm a dying breed is incorrect, because I don't think anybody has ever thrown like me. I'm not tooting my own horn. The way I play, my mechanics are the worst you've ever seen when you're watching on TV or on film. But you can't argue with production."

—The Associated Press,
December 20, 2003

"If I was a fan, I would love watching me play. Not because I'm a picture-perfect passer like Joe Montana. I have so much fun playing that the fans in the stands are probably wondering, 'What's he going to do this time?' I like to watch certain players in games. You know somebody's going to do something you want to see replayed, then watch it again the next day on *SportsCenter*. I'm that type of player. I think people love that."

—Dallas Morning News,
December 31, 1995

"I expect to be in the Hall of Fame. But mostly I hope that in 20 or 30 years people will say, 'That goddamn Favre, you had to watch yourself around him. He'd throw ice or put something in your jock, but on Sunday that son of a bitch was ready to play.'"

—Playboy,
November 1997

HIS SUCCESS

"Nobody knows how hard it is to get to the top and how hard it is to stay on top."

—Esquire,
October 1996

"It's hard to believe I've achieved as much as I have, for a kid who just wanted to dress in an NFL uniform. If I was to outline my career, what it would be like or what I would want it to be like, I couldn't even come close to what I've achieved."

—Wisconsin State Journal,
September 29, 2002

HIS WIFE, DEANNA

"She has been there every single time I needed her. Somebody wondered why I didn't sign a prenuptial. You know what, after all the shit Deanna's had to go through with me, she's entitled to half of everything.

—Esquire,
October 1996

ON CENTER FRANK WINTERS

"My hands are under Frank's butt a hundred times a day. I have a unique job, and so does he."

—Esquire,
October 1996

Commenting on what it would be like to play with a different center:
"I would be nervous. I'm so used to his butt now it's kind of molded around my hand. …That's kind of the way I am with Frank. I don't want to take a snap from anyone else. And I'm sure it would feel funny for another quarterback to come in and start feeling around up in there."

—Packer Plus,
December 18, 1996

ON COACH MIKE HOLMGREN

During a time-out in a cold game against the Raiders:
"Mike, you've got a frozen shield of snot all over your damn mustache."

—Esquire,
October 1996

FOOTBALL

"It's a good game for someone who will go out and knock himself silly to get a win."

—Playboy,
November 1997

ENDING HIS CAREER

"I'm just a good old Southern boy from South Mississippi who dreamed of playing football some day, and my dream came true. And I have not cheated myself or my teammates or the fans one bit about my work ethic, my preparation and the way I play this game. I only play it one way. I only practice it one way, and that's the only way I'll ever do it. If that ever changes, I will leave this game immediately."

—Biloxi Sun Herald,
November 8, 1999

"When it counts, I still think I'm the best. And that keeps me kicking myself in the butt and being not quite ready to leave yet."

—USA Today,
February 20, 2004

"I feel fine. My arm and throwing's not the problem. It's everything else. The reason I'm standing here today is I can still throw with the best of them. There's no doubt about that. But putting my socks on in the morning, that's the tough part. Once I get up, get loose and get moving, which takes a lot longer than it used to, I'm fine."

—Milwaukee Journal Sentinel,
June 10, 2004

MISCELLANEOUS

On being traded to Green Bay:
"Probably the best thing ever to happen to me was that I went out and partied, drank a lot of beer, didn't show up for meetings on time and got traded. I hate to say that, but it got me out of Atlanta."

—Sport,
November 1995

Favre Quotes

On Packer Mark Chmura, a conservative Republican, boycotting the Packers' visit to the White House to meet President Clinton after the 1996 Super Bowl win:
"Mark was pissing into the wind. We all got on him for it. We all said, 'Right, Chmura, like the White House gives a shit. The president is losing sleep because he won't get to meet Mark Chmura.' I think Mark missed something good. We got to see where the president works and putts."
—Playboy,
November 1997

Reacting to Minneapolis radio disc jockey who reported that Favre didn't stay in a room on the same floor of a hotel as his teammates before a Vikings game in Minnesota:
"It's (expletive). (Expletive) anybody who prints it."
—Milwaukee Journal Sentinel,
December 1, 1997

The idea of playing for Vince Lombardi:
"I don't know. He probably would have killed me by now. But I would love to play one game for the guy. I know I have the toughness."
—The Charlotte Observer,
January 10, 1997

Learning to be an NFL quarterback:
"My first couple of years in Green Bay I realized I was doing the hardest thing in sports. We had 16 quarterback meetings a week. Learning our offense—any pro offense, really—is harder than learning chemistry or calculus."
—Sports Illustrated,
October 14, 1996

On a tape of his seven interceptions in two games in 2002:
"Great, now let's put on a tape of my 20 touchdown passes."
—Milwaukee Journal Sentinel,
December 2, 2002

On Packer George Teague's 101-yard interception return for a touchdown, a post-season record:
"I was so happy, me and Frank Winters was swapping spit."
—Los Angeles Times,
January 9, 1994

QUOTES BY OTHERS

"Favre is a pickup-truck, six-pack-of-beer quarterback. Maybe two six-packs."

—Rick Gosselin, *Dallas Morning News*,
December 31, 1995

"The biggest star of the chilly and efficient NFL is Green Bay's Brett Favre, all flash and daring as a quarterback, a reckless onetime pill popper and a scion of a family that apparently has rampaged through rural Mississippi like a passel of redneck Kennedys."

—Charles Pierce, *Esquire*,
September 1997

"I've seen him pick up a baseball with his feet."

—John Madden, in broadcast
of Super Bowl XXXI

"He ages me every day. He also gives me great joy. It's kind of like one of my kids. I'm just glad he doesn't live with me."

—Mike Holmgren, *Minneapolis Star Tribune*,
January 5, 1998

"You want to know the best part of the Favre package? Of all of the superstars in the NFL today, Favre cares the least about the attention he is due. He doesn't want it; he doesn't need it. He is genuinely a good person."

—Joe Buck, *The Sporting News*,
January 26, 2004

"Ever since the Lombardi years (I am 63), I have intensely disliked the Green Bay Packers—even when they were losing, I detested them. But, of late, Brett has made me a fan of those green and gold bleeps. In fact, he's about the only reason to even watch the NFL anymore. I love the way he appears to be having fun in the moment. No premeditated 'celebrations' with Sharpies and cell phones, just apparently the joy of competing and doing it very well. I'll be sad when he hangs 'em up (and will probably hang mine up, too)."

—Tom Halleck, letter to the editor in
The Orlando Sentinel, December 28, 2003

"He was a crazy, wild country boy."

—Greg Blache, former Packers assistant coach,
The Sporting News, November 1996

"Brett is very much like a psychopath in the sense that he has no conscience. He's able to forget bad things. He's able to forget the good things."

—Tom Jackson of ESPN,
Milwaukee Journal Sentinel, December 2, 2002

"When we'd drive to practice, Brett would be in the back of a truck, and Brett would moon people. Or a bunch of us would be sitting in the Jacuzzi in the training room and he would dive in belly-flop style. Or maybe he'll catch Reggie White daydreaming just long enough to dump a bucket of ice water over his head. Or he'll put shaving cream inside the earpiece of a phone and tell a rookie he has a call."

—Former Packer Terrell Buckley,
The Sporting News, November 18, 1996

"He's a character. He does things that'll make you shake your head sometimes. And he does things that'll make you hold your nose sometimes."

—Packer Reggie White,
The Charlotte Observer, January 10, 1997

"No player in the NFL identifies or is more closely linked to a specific team like Brett Favre is to the Green Bay Packers.

"He embodies the spirit and character of Packer fans everywhere. I do not think there is a player in the NFL that experiences a relationship with the fans like Brett Favre does.

"That is very, very special."

—Packers Head Coach Mike Sherman

Favre doing his first-ever Lambeau Leap after scoring a touchdown on October 29, 2006, against the Arizona Cardinals.

MPP
MOST POPULAR PLAYER

✫✫✫✫✫✫✫✫✫✫

Even late in his career, Brett Favre remained one of the most popular professional athletes in any sport.

In 2006, Favre:

- Was ranked the fourth most popular athlete in America—in all sports—according to a Harris Poll.

- Had the fifth-highest "Q rating" among all sports figures, as measured by his familiarity and likeability among consumers, according to *SportsBusiness Journal.*

- Was ranked the 89th "Greatest American" in a nationwide vote of more than a half-million viewers of The Discovery Channel.

- Was ranked No. 1 in the book, *Pain Gang: Pro Football's Fifty Toughest Players.* Wrote author Neil Reynolds: "His consecutive starts streak is very impressive. Add in the fact that he has spent close to 40 weeks of his career on Green Bay's injury list but never missed a game, and the sure-fire Hall of Famer's feats become truly amazing."

STATS
AND
NOTES

✶✶✶✶✶✶✶✶✶✶

PASSING STATS

Year	Team	G	GS	Att	Comp	Pct	Yds	YPA	Lg	TD	Int	Tkld	20+	40+	Rate
1991	Atlanta	2	0	4	0	0.0	0	0.00	0	0	2	1/11	0	0	0.0
1992	Green Bay	15	13	471	302	64.1	3227	6.85	76	18	13	34/208	30	9	85.3
1993	Green Bay	16	16	522	318	60.9	3303	6.33	66	19	24	30/199	37	5	72.2
1994	Green Bay	16	16	582	363	62.4	3882	6.67	49	33	14	31/188	44	4	90.7
1995	Green Bay	16	16	570	359	63.0	4413	7.74	99	38	13	33/217	59	5	99.5
1996	Green Bay	16	16	543	325	59.9	3899	7.18	80	39	13	40/241	49	11	95.8
1997	Green Bay	16	16	513	304	59.3	3867	7.54	74	35	16	25/176	61	9	92.6
1998	Green Bay	16	16	551	347	63.0	4212	7.64	84	31	23	38/223	47	9	87.8
1999	Green Bay	16	16	595	341	57.3	4091	6.88	74	22	23	35/223	52	11	74.7
2000	Green Bay	16	16	580	338	58.3	3812	6.57	67	20	16	33/236	41	7	78.0
2001	Green Bay	16	16	510	314	61.6	3921	7.69	67	32	15	22/151	53	13	94.1
2002	Green Bay	16	16	551	341	61.9	3658	6.64	85	27	16	26/188	39	7	85.6
2003	Green Bay	16	16	471	308	65.4	3361	7.14	66	32	21	19/137	42	7	90.4
2004	Green Bay	16	16	540	346	64.1	4088	7.57	79	30	17	12/93	50	12	92.4
2005	Green Bay	16	16	607	372	61.3	3881	6.39	59	20	29	24/170	40	7	70.9
2006	Green Bay	16	16	613	343	56.0	3885	6.34	82	18	18	21/134	49	8	72.7
Total		**241**	**237**	**8223**	**5021**	**61.1**	**57500**	**6.99**	**99**	**414**	**273**	**424/2795**	**693**	**124**	**85.1**

Source: NFL.com

PLAYOFFS

Year	Team	GP	GS	Att	Comp	Pct	Yds	Att	TD	Int	Lg	Sk	Lst	Rating
1993	Green Bay	2	2	71	43	60.6	535	7.5	5	3	48	2	4	89.8
1994	Green Bay	2	2	73	41	56.2	473	6.5	0	1	59	2	15	70.2
1995	Green Bay	3	3	102	66	64.7	805	7.9	8	2	73t	6	41	106.9
1996	Green Bay	3	3	71	44	62.0	617	8.7	5	1	81t	7	60	107.5
1997	Green Bay	3	3	97	56	57.7	668	6.9	5	3	40	6	23	83.2
1998	Green Bay	1	1	35	20	57.1	292	8.3	2	2	47	1	10	79.7
2001	Green Bay	2	2	73	48	65.8	550	7.5	4	7	51	3	23	67.0
2002	Green Bay	1	1	42	20	47.6	247	5.9	1	2	37	2	14	54.4
2003	Green Bay	2	2	66	41	62.1	499	7.6	3	1	44	1	9	94.2
2004	Green Bay	1	1	33	22	66.7	216	6.5	1	4	28	2	15	55.4
	Postseason (10 years)	20	20	663	401	60.5	4,902	7.4	34	26	81t	32	214	84.0

Career postseason record as starter: 11-9 (.550).
Source: Packers.com

RUSHING

Year	Team	G	GS	Att	Yds	Avg	Lg	TD	20+	1st
1991	Atlanta	2	0	0	0	---	0	0	0	0
1992	Green Bay	15	13	47	198	4.2	19	1	0	11
1993	Green Bay	16	16	58	216	3.7	27	1	2	13
1994	Green Bay	16	16	42	202	4.8	36	2	3	14
1995	Green Bay	16	16	39	181	4.6	40	3	2	17
1996	Green Bay	16	16	49	136	2.8	23	2	1	18
1997	Green Bay	16	16	58	187	3.2	16	1	0	16
1998	Green Bay	16	16	40	133	3.3	35	1	1	13
1999	Green Bay	16	16	28	142	5.1	20	0	1	11
2000	Green Bay	16	16	27	108	4.0	18	0	0	7
2001	Green Bay	16	16	38	56	1.5	14	1	0	5
2002	Green Bay	16	16	25	73	2.9	17	0	0	6
2003	Green Bay	16	16	18	15	0.8	7	0	0	3
2004	Green Bay	16	16	16	36	2.3	17	0	0	2
2005	Green Bay	16	16	18	62	3.4	20	0	1	4
2006	Green Bay	16	16	23	29	1.3	14	1	0	4
Total		**241**	**237**	**526**	**1774**	**3.4**	**40**	**13**	**11**	**144**

Source: NFL.com

CAREER DEFENSIVE STATS

Year	Team	G	Total	Tkl	Ast	Sacks	Int	Yds	Avg	Lg	TD	Pass Def
1991	Atlanta	2	0	0.0	0	0	0	0	0.0	0	0	0
1992	Green Bay	15	1	1.0	0	0	0	0	0.0	0	0	0
1993	Green Bay	16	4	4.0	0	0	0	0	0.0	0	0	0
1994	Green Bay	16	2	2.0	0	0	0	0	0.0	0	0	0
1995	Green Bay	16	2	2.0	0	0	0	0	0.0	0	0	0
1996	Green Bay	16	1	1.0	0	0	0	0	0.0	0	0	0
1997	Green Bay	16	0	0.0	0	0	0	0	0.0	0	0	0
1998	Green Bay	16	0	0.0	0	0	0	0	0.0	0	0	0
1999	Green Bay	16	1	1.0	0	0	0	0	0.0	0	0	0
2000	Green Bay	16	1	1.0	0	0	0	0	0.0	0	0	0
2001	Green Bay	16	0	0.0	0	0	0	0	0.0	0	0	0
2002	Green Bay	16	3	2.0	1	0	0	0	0.0	0	0	0
2003	Green Bay	16	1	1.0	0	0	0	0	0.0	0	0	0
2004	Green Bay	16	0	0.0	0	0	0	0	0.0	0	0	0
2005	Green Bay	16	2	2.0	0	0	0	0	0.0	0	0	0
2006	Green Bay	16	0	0.0	0	0	0	0	0.0	0	0	0
Total		**241**	**18**	**17.0**	**1**	**0**	**0**	**0**	**0.0**	**0**	**0**	**0**

Source: NFL.com

FAVRE'S PERSONAL RECORDS

Through 2006 season

NFL RECORDS

MOST CONSECUTIVE GAMES STARTED, QUARTERBACK:
237 (257 including post-season)

MOST CONSECUTIVE STARTS WITHOUT A SHUTOUT:
222

MOST COMPLETIONS, CAREER:
5,021

**MOST SEASONS (AND MOST CONSECUTIVE SEASONS)
WITH 3,000-PLUS PASSING YARDS:**
15 (1992–2006)

MOST SEASONS WITH 30-PLUS TOUCHDOWN PASSES:
8

**MOST CONSECUTIVE SEASONS WITH
20-PLUS TOUCHDOWN PASSES:**
12 (1994–2005)

MOST SEASONS LEADING LEAGUE IN TOUCHDOWN PASSES:
4 (1995-1997, 2003; record shared with
Johnny Unitas, Len Dawson, and Steve Young)

MOST CONSECUTIVE GAMES WITH TOUCHDOWN PASS, POST-SEASON:
16 (1995–2004)

LONGEST PASS COMPLETION:
99 yards (Robert Brooks, vs. Chicago Bears,
September 11, 1995; record shared with several other players)

MOST CONSECUTIVE SEASONS WITH 8 OR MORE VICTORIES:
13 (1995–2004)

HIGH COMPLETION PERCENTAGE AMONG
LEADERS IN PASSING ATTEMPTS:
61.1% (Dan Marino, 59.4; Warren Moon, 58.4; Drew Bledsoe, 57.2;
Fran Tarkenton, 57.0; John Elway, 56.9)

SINGLE-STADIUM CAREER TOUCHDOWN PASSES:
195

Favre ranks in the top three for these NFL records:
MOST TOUCHDOWN PASSES, CAREER:
Second (414), behind Marino (420)

MOST PASSING YARDS, CAREER:
Second (57,500), behind Marino (61,361)

MOST VICTORIES AS STARTING QUARTERBACK:
Tied for second (147–90–0, .620) with Marino (147–93–0, .613),
behind Elway (148–82–1, .643)

MOST CONSECUTIVE GAMES WITH TOUCHDOWN PASS:
Second (36, 2002–'04), behind Johnny Unitas (47, 1956–'60)

MOST GAMES WITH 4 OR MORE TOUCHDOWN PASSES:
Second (19), behind Marino (21)

MOST PASSING ATTEMPTS, CAREER:
Second (8,224), behind Marino (8,358)

MOST TOUCHDOWN PASSES, POST-SEASON:
Second (8,224), behind Marino (8,358)

MOST PASSING YARDS, POST-SEASON:
Third (4,902), behind Joe Montana (5,773) and Elway (4,964)

MOST CONSECUTIVE GAMES STARTED, ANY POSITION:
Third (237), behind Jim Marshall (270) and Mick Tingelhoff (240)

SINGLE-GAME PERSONAL BESTS

ATTEMPTS
61 vs. San Francisco, October 14, 1996

COMPLETIONS
36 at Chicago, December 5, 1993

PASSING YARDS
402 at Chicago, December 5, 1993

COMPLETION PERCENTAGE*
82.1 at Cleveland, November 19, 1995

TOUCHDOWN PASSES
5 vs. Chicago, November 12, 1995

INTERCEPTIONS
5 at Cincinnati, October 30, 2005

PASSER RATING*
154.9 at Oakland, December 22, 2003

LONGEST PASS
99 yards at Chicago, September 11, 1995

LONGEST RUN
40 yards at Jacksonville, September 24, 1995

* Minimum 20 attempts

MISCELLANEOUS

- Second team NFL All-Decade Team for '90s as chosen by Pro Football Hall of Fame Selection Committee.

- Pro Bowl selection: 1992, 1993, 1995, 1996, 1997, 2001, 2002

- Only NFL player to win Most Valuable Player award three years (shared it with Barry Sanders in 1997). In 2002, runner-up to Oakland Raiders quarterback Rich Gannon; that year, named MVP by *Dallas Morning News* and player of the year by *Sports Illustrated.*

- Only athlete in the four major sports to have started every game for the same team since September 27, 1992 (through 2006).

Source: Packers.com

INDEX

★★★★★★★★★★★

Author Tom Kertscher and Packers team photographer Jim Biever on Lambeau Field during the Minnesota Vikings game on December 21, 2006.

ABOUT THE AUTHOR

Tom Kertscher, a Wisconsin native, has worked as a local news reporter and editor since graduating from the University of Wisconsin-Madison in 1984. He worked for newspapers in Oklahoma, Illinois, and California, and he received a master's degree in journalism from Ohio State University before joining the *Milwaukee Journal Sentinel* in 1998.

Brett Favre: A Packer Fan's Tribute is Tom Kertscher's second book. For the second time, Kertscher has honored one of the icons of Wisconsin sports. His first book, *Cracked Sidewalks and French Pastry: The Wit and Wisdom of Al McGuire* (University of Wisconsin Press, 2003), is a collection of quotations uttered by the late Marquette University basketball coach and broadcaster.

Tom is thankful that his dad, Jim, bought Packers season tickets in the 1960s and never gave them up.

He lives in Milwaukee with his daughter, Hailey.